# StampCraft

Dozens of creative ideas for stamping
on cards, clothing, furniture and more

## Cari Haysom

Chilton Book Company
Radnor, Pennsylvania

**A Quarto Book**

Copyright © 1996 Quarto Inc.

All rights reserved.
First published in the United States by
Chilton Book Company, Radnor, Pennsylvania

ISBN 1-8019-8850-0

A CIP record for this book is available from the Library of Congress

This book was designed and produced by
Quarto Publishing plc
The Old Brewery
6 Blundell Street
London N7 9BH

**Senior editors** Anna Selby, Eileen Cadman, Miranda Stonor
**Senior art editor** Clare Baggaley
**Designer** Vicki James
**Illustrator** Neil Ballpit
**Photographers** Sandy Porter, Chas Wilder
**Art director** Moira Clinch
**Editorial director** Mark Dartford

Typeset by Central Southern Typesetters, Eastbourne
Manufactured in Singapore by CH Colour Scan SDN BHD
Printed in Singapore by Star Standard Industries (Pte) Ltd

# CONTENTS

# INTRODUCTION

The impulse to decorate the home and objects of daily use has existed since prehistoric man adorned his caves and the Egyptians and the Romans painted their walls and artefacts. Originally the preserve of the nobility, ornamentation throughout history has flourished – from the block-printed seals of ancient Babylon to the opulence of the Renaissance and the inventive naiveté of colonial America's itinerant decorators. Through the ages, ingenious techniques were employed for the less affluent as they sought to acquire the same elegantly decorated furnishings, creating decorative techniques of wit and imagination. As designs crossed the social divide, so styles crossed country boundaries. Influences of Europe can be found in colonial America, while traditional designs from Africa, South America, and the Far East adorn homes in Europe and North America.

No longer the preserve of the specialist, decorating the home is within the reach of all enthusiasts, and the stamp is one of the most versatile and innovative ways of instant decorating. With beautiful and intricate manufactured stamps, or even the humble potato, you can create a design of quiet elegance or bold simplicity.

From stamping a special card to a loved one, to decorating an entire room, from the curtains to the wastepaper basket, there is nothing too small or too large to be stamped. If you have a sudden whim to brighten up a gloomy bathroom, just grab the sponge and get stamping. On a wet day, get the children stamping, too.

The combination of paint techniques and stamping extends the effects so that almost any style can be achieved, from a distressed "antique" firescreen to a high-gloss lacquer finish. Whatever your style, stamping is guaranteed to accommodate and embellish it.

# STAMPS

*The art of stamping couldn't be easier. You simply apply ink or paint to a pre-carved image and print it onto a chosen surface. With stamps you can be as creative as you please. Whether you use a manufactured stamp and arrange and color them in your own way or whether you design your own homemade stamp, the finished result will be unique to you.*

### MANUFACTURED RUBBER STAMPS

There are a wealth of beautiful designs in manufactured rubber stamps – intricate patterns, flowers, animals, toys, and calligraphy. With the use of a variety of different paints and inks, they can be used to print on paper and cardboard, fabric, ceramics, and even walls – so you can transform every aspect of your home. Before choosing your stamp, consider what you are going to print on. Small, very detailed stamps can look lost on a large article. On the other hand, if you want to stamp onto a curved surface, a large stamp will be difficult to manipulate. Take care of your stamps and they will last for years.

### HOMEMADE STAMPS

#### Sponge stamps

A very effective stamp can be made from an ordinary bath sponge or upholstery foam. The density of the sponge or foam will determine the textural pattern of your print. For simple shapes, such as a heart or star, a medium-density sponge is best and adds an interesting texture. For a motif with more detail, for instance a bird with beak and feathers, a high-density sponge would be preferable.

#### Styrofoam stamps

Plain untextured styrofoam tiles are another good material for making your own stamps. They can be purchased from most hardware stores. There are expensive tools for cutting foam, but you can make an effective homemade tool from a sewing needle embedded in a bottle cork, heated over a household candle. Mount the stamp on hardboard after you have cut it out. You can make quite small stamps from styrofoam, though they will have only a limited amount of detail.

#### Eraser stamps

For simple borders and tiny motifs, an ordinary eraser is perfect. It is easy to cut and gives a smooth even print. The only limitations are the sizes of the erasers on the market. You can draw or trace a design straight onto the eraser and cut it out with a craft knife – the amount of detail depends on individual cutting skills.

#### Potato stamps

Perhaps the most basic of stamps – but still enormously effective and not to be spurned – is the humble potato. The trick is to keep to something simple and make sure that, when initially cutting the potato in half, the surface is straight, and not cut diagonally so that only half the motif prints. A good clean chop usually works. It will keep for several days in a fridge, wrapped in a paper bag.

### CARE OF STAMPS

In order to maintain a clear image and extend the life of your stamps, you must take good care of them. Never leave them uncleaned after use. Some manufactured stamps come with their own cleaner which effectively cleans off all inks and paints. Alternatively, use a mixture of liquid detergent and water, or water and window cleaner. If paint has been allowed to dry on the stamps, scrub them gently with an old toothbrush. Never use harsh detergents or immerse in water. To store, place them upside down (rubber side down) and keep them out of direct sunlight. Make sure your stamps are cleaned well between printing different colors. Some inks will stain the rubber, but this won't affect the quality of the prints. Styrofoam and eraser stamps should be cleaned in the same way, but won't stand up to extensive cleaning or scrubbing. Sponges should be washed in clean water. Potatoes should be wiped clean with a wet cloth.

# INKS AND PAINTS

*Choosing the appropriate ink or paint for stamping and decorative work involves three considerations. First, consider the type of surface you are decorating – whether it is wood, fabric, or ceramic. Second, think about the effect you wish to achieve – a delicate, crisp image or, alternatively, one that is bold and vibrant. Third, consider how much wear and tear your finished article will receive.*

## INKS

Most stamp manufacturers supply their own brand of inks, inked pads, and special felt-tip pens for use with stamps. It is important always to check the instructions as their suitability for different surfaces can vary. Basically there are two types of inks: inked pads and felt tips.

**Pigment pads**, bought already inked with a water-based pigment, and **water-based felt-tip pens** are suitable for printing on paper and for embossing on any surface. They are slow drying and can be washed out of material before embossing if you make a mistake.

**Fabric inks** and **fabric ink felt-tip pens** are permanent, quick drying, and non-toxic. When stamped onto fabric, they are washable and require no heat setting. They can be used on most surfaces, except ceramics, but you can't stamp pale colors onto dark surfaces. Fabric inks come in bottles, and they can be used with ink pads or can be rubbed directly onto the stamps.

Fabric ink felt-tip pens are extremely versatile. They can be used to draw or color directly onto fabrics, to apply several different colors to a stamp before printing, to color a stamped print for découpage, and to add color to a print on most surfaces. Like the fabric inks, pale colors do not show up on a dark surface.

**Embossing ink** is a clear – some brands are tinted – ink used only with embossing powders. Using a foam-backed pad, the image is stamped in the usual way. A metallic powder is sprinkled on top and heat is applied with a heat gun to melt the powder, creating a metallic sparkling print. Pigment ink can also be used, as it is slow drying, and the color of the ink is invisible once the powder melts, when you use gold, silver, or bronze powder.

## PAINTS

**Acrylic paints** are water-based paints that have many uses in decorative printing. They can be applied to stamps with a small roller, a brush or, in the case of homemade stamps, you just dip them in. Using an acrylic fabric medium, they can be used on most fabrics. They are also suitable for stamping on wood, walls, and for stamping pale colors onto dark backgrounds. In a number of the smaller projects in this book, they have been used as a base color. As they dry quickly, any mistakes must be wiped off immediately with a damp cloth, and brushes and stamps should not be allowed to dry. Always mix the amount you need and *no more* – if you need to mix the same color again, note the quantities you use. A useful hint – particularly if you like a color you've mixed – is to paint it onto a small piece of cardboard and write the colors you used and the exact amount on the back. Keep these cards in a box for future reference.

**Artist's oil paints** are useful for tinting varnishes, glazes, and decorator's oil paints. They are thinned with turpentine or mineral spirits. Clean the brushes afterward with mineral spirits.

**Decorator's oil paints** are useful for larger projects that are likely to have a lot of wear. These oil-based paints come in gloss, silk matte, and flat finishes, though gloss is unsuitable for stamping and for paint finishes. For use in decorative finishes, flat white oil paint is by far the best, as it is softer than the other paints, making it excellent for fine sanding and for antique finishes. If this is not readily available, a silk or matte finish is perfectly adequate. Decorator's oil paints come in a legion of colors. If you are planning to decorate a number of small articles, it is a good idea to buy one large can of white paint and, using artist's oil paints, mix your own colors. Blend the artist's oil colors with a little mineral spirits until they are smooth and add to the white paint little by little. Experiment – it saves buying dozens of different colors. Clean your brushes and thin the paint, if necessary, with mineral spirits.

**Latex paint** is water based and available in a flat, silk, or satin finish. It is suitable for painting on all surfaces, but it is too absorbent for most decorative paint finishes. It can be used for stamping with sponges onto an latex-painted surface, but not with any other stamps. Clean brushes and thin the paint, if necessary, with water.

**Fabric paints** are simple to use and easily set and washable. It is important to buy paints for printing and not for painting, as the latter are too runny for stamping. Colors of the same brand can be mixed to obtain the exact color you need. Always read the manufacturer's instructions before use to check whether or not heat setting is necessary. Fabric paints can be used on most materials. The results, however, can vary so it is always wise to practice stamping on a scrap first. On heavy textured fabric, a delicately detailed stamp will be all but lost. On the other hand, a simple potato print could look wonderfully primitive or antique. Acrylic fabric paints with fabric medium produce vibrant colors and are the most successful for stamping pale colors on a dark background. Fabric inks are best on fine paler shades of material where a crisp, detailed image is required.

**Ceramic paints** have opened up the field of decorative ceramics for those without access to a kiln. It must be remembered, however, that they are purely for decorative use and *not* utilitarian. Furthermore, while they can be washed gently, they will not stand up to dishwashers or vigorous scrubbing.

Water-based ceramic paints dry in about four hours and, after 24 hours, their durability is improved by hardening off in a home oven. Always read the manufacturer's instructions to check the recommended time in the oven. If the temperature is too high, the colors will develop a brown tinge, but if it is too low, the paint will not harden properly and will flake off. Cold ceramic paints come in a variety of colors which can be mixed with one another to make other colors.

Solvent-based ceramic paints, those diluted with mineral spirits, have a wider range of colors than the water-based ones and come with a clear varnish which will provide added protection to the finished decoration.

Homemade sponge stamps are probably the easiest way to stamp onto ceramics, particularly as they fit easily around curves and don't slip on a glazed surface. However, it is possible to stamp manufactured stamps onto ceramics (see the cup and saucer on page 96). One way of dealing with the shiny surface is to paint the item first, leave to dry, and then stamp on top using a small stamp.

**Gold paints** vary considerably from a yellow, almost brassy look, to a brownish-tinged gold which can look quite murky. The acrylic selection is generally very good. Antique gold is a soft pale color while renaissance gold is stronger and darker. In the end, it is largely a matter of preference. An alternative is to use gold metallic powder mixed into white glue. The glue is transparent and, when dry, leaves a glowing gold. Mix 2 tablespoons of glue to 1 tablespoon of water, adding 1 teaspoon of gold metallic powder. This mixture can be used for stamping or for painting stamped motifs for use as découpage.

**Gold felt-tip pens** are used for lining or striping, to enhance the contours and the decorative detail in painted furniture with a line close to the edge. You will need a permanent-type ink which is solvent-based and, if the piece requires varnishing afterward, apply a coat of French polish as a barrier first. Gold felt-tip pens come in various sizes: fine, medium and large.

# FINISHES

*A basic knowledge of the various finishes, whether for protective purposes or for solely decorative use, is essential. When using specialist varnishes and paints, always read the manufacturer's instructions.*

## VARNISHES AND GLAZES

**Modern polyurethane varnishes** are easy to apply and less likely to yellow than they used to be. They come in several finishes – gloss, semi-matte, matte, and flat. In decorative painting, a flat varnish followed by a coat of

good-quality furniture polish gives greater depth and richness than a high-gloss finish. Matte and flat varnishes are softer than gloss, so if the item being decorated is likely to receive a lot of wear, first apply a coat of gloss and, when dry, sand it lightly and apply a coat of flat varnish. When a really shiny surface is required, apply several coats of gloss sanding in between.

**Glazes** are not to be confused with varnishes, which are principally used to give a protective coating. Glazes are slower drying, semi-transparent films of oil color used to give an antique patina and a depth and subtlety to colors. Transparent oil glaze or "scumble glaze" is available from most good paint stores. It can be tinted with artist's oil colors and should always be a couple of tones darker than the base color. For an antique patina, the glaze can be brushed over the surface, left to dry, and sanded to reveal patches of the undercolor, or it can be stippled or sponged on before being sanded. Alternatively, it can be painted on and wiped off unevenly while still wet. For subtle color effects, apply a tinted glaze evenly over a colored base and leave to dry. Experiment with pale colors over a white base, a darker hue of the same color, or a contrasting color.

**Shellac** comes in various colors from white to orange and is most frequently used in **French polishing**. French polish – refined shellac – can be used as a barrier between different stages of work and in a facsimile of lacquer work. Soluble in denatured alcohol, it dries quickly (about an hour) and is impervious to most solvents. Applying French polish requires a certain amount of skill and dexterity as it starts to dry immediately and going over the same area twice produces a patchy effect. It should be applied in one clean sweep. The simplest way is with a soft, lint-free cloth dipped into the French polish.

**Water-based pickling paste** can be painted over a colored base or plain wood, left to dry, then rubbed off to reveal the color and wood grain underneath. For the best effect, apply it to surfaces that have a marked wood grain. Do not varnish, as this will ruin the chalky effect.

**Translucent paint** is a water-based paint for wood that does not obscure the wood grain. It works just as effectively on painted wood, revealing but slightly changing the color underneath. Whereas pickling paste produces a somewhat dry chalky finish, white translucent paint gives a delicate, almost pearly finish.

**French enamel varnish** comes in brilliant colors in a shellac solution. Soluble in denatured alcohol, it dries rapidly so you have to work quickly.

**Crackleglaze varnish** is a specialist varnish used only for the technique of crackle glazing. It is applied between two coats of water-based paints. After the first coat of paint has dried, the crackleglaze varnish is applied, left to dry completely, then the second coat of paint is applied, which "crackles" to reveal the first coat of paint.

## CLEANERS AND ABRASIVES

**Mineral spirits** dilutes all oil-based paints and most varnishes as well as cleaning brushes and utensils.

**Denatured alcohol** dilutes all shellac-based derivatives.

**Wet and dry sandpaper**, an abrasive paper, not only levels the surface, but provides "tooth" for subsequent coats of paint or varnish. It is available in different grits – coarse, medium, fine, and very fine. As indicated, it can be used dry (as it is) or wet, with a solution of water and non-detergent soap.

**Steel wool** does a similar job and comes in the same grades from coarse through to very fine. It is more efficient than sandpaper for sanding curves.

# EQUIPMENT

*The first temptation is to buy all the "right gear." Certainly an investment in a few good brushes is vital, but no decorator should be without an assortment of "bits and bobs" – you will discover new uses for them all.*

### BRUSHES

Brushes come in a wide variety of shapes and sizes, and can be made from different kinds of hair.

**Standard decorator's brushes** made from bristle are used for painting walls and woodwork. Specialized oval brushes can be bought for varnishing. However, a decorator's brush is quite suitable if it is kept only for varnishing. A 1in. (2.5cm) decorator's brush is a good basic brush for painting furniture.

**Artist's brushes,** for oil painting, watercolors, and acrylic are essential for decorative paintwork. They also come in a variety of shapes and sizes made from different hair. Flat bristle brushes, ending in a straight edge delivering long broad strokes, and round bristle brushes, with rounded edges giving a smoother effect, are the most useful, ranging from sizes 6–10.

**Fine sable brushes** are useful for delicate work. They have extremely fine points and are both strong and flexible, allowing precise control over the paint. They are, however, very expensive. Synthetic hair was introduced due to the expense of sable and is particularly suitable for acrylics, as it mimics natural hair and bristle. They come in the same shapes and sizes. Another useful brush, suitable for stippling, is the **fitch**, a name loosely applied to oversized brushes with cut ends.

For dragging, traditionally a **flogger** is the correct brush. However, for small projects a standard decorator's brush is perfectly adequate.

**Care of brushes** is important. Always clean your brushes after use. If they are used for oil-based paints and varnishes, clean them with mineral spirits or a commercial cleaner and wrap in paper secured with a rubber band to keep the bristles from splaying out. Brushes used for latex and acrylics should be washed in soap and warm water or a commercial cleaner.

**Small rollers** designed for painting woodwork are ideal for applying paint to stamps. They are usually made from sponge foam. Clean them in the same way as the brushes.

### KNIVES, MATS, AND PAPER

**Craft knives** are small, light knives with blades that snap off when they are blunt. They are used for cutting out stamped prints for cards and découpage. Buy one that comes with spare blades and a device for snapping and storing the blades safely. Alternatively, you can use a craft scalpel. The sharp, fine blades can be replaced when they are blunt. They come in a variety of shapes – the best is short and triangular in profile, with a sharp point. Always take care with spare and used blades.

**A cutting mat** is a flexible rubber board, invaluable for cutting out paper motifs with a craft knife. It holds paper securely, and prevents it from slipping while cutting. Even more importantly, it prevents the knife from slipping.

**Handmade paper** is readily available in most good art and craft stores. Blank cards made from recycled cotton come in various colors. **Mulberry paper** is made from the bark of the mulberry tree. It comes in a range of lovely colors and is ideal for stamping.

### ADHESIVES

**Repositioning glue** comes in a spray can or as a small stick. It allows you to glue stamped motifs temporarily, then remove them, when working out a design. It should not be left on indefinitely or used to stick motifs down permanently.

**All-purpose craft glue** appears in many forms. Buy one that dries clear, is safe and non-toxic, and is simple to use. You should also check that it glues the type of materials you will be using.

**White glue and sealer** is a glue that has other uses in decorative painting and stamping. In the projects on pages 86 and 94, it is mixed with gold metallic powder and used in the same way as a paint. It dries clear, leaving the gold powder adhering to the surface.

**Wood glue** is used specifically for wood and is suitable for joints under continual stress.

**Masking tape** is a self-adhesive tape used in decorating to protect edges while painting. It can be used to blank out certain areas while adjacent areas are painted and helps to paint a crisp, straight edge.

**Masking paper** is a transparent film of self-adhesive paper, often used to protect documents and books. It can be used in place of masking tape, the advantage being that it can be cut to size and shape.

## HEAT SOURCES

**A heat gun** is a small tool which most stamp manufacturers sell for embossing. It heats the metallic powder without burning or blowing it, and is safe to use. Although some heat guns look like a small hairdryer, you should never use a hairdryer. An alternative source of heat which will melt the powder, albeit more slowly, is a toaster. Hold the image a couple of inches *above* the toaster until the powder melts. *Never* attempt to put it inside the toaster.

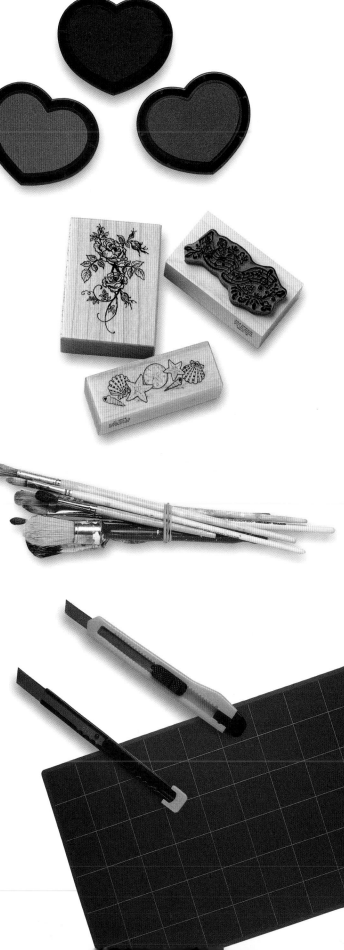

# USING INK, PAINT, AND COLORINGS

*T*he way in which color is applied to stamps determines the final effect of your print. Too much ink or paint will produce a blotchy image, whereas too little will make the image look faint.

## INKING THE PAD

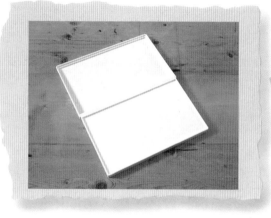

**1** Always use a clean pad before you begin stamping, to ensure a clear print.

**2** Pour the ink onto the pad and massage it in well until it is completely covered. Always keep the lid closed when you are not using the pad or the ink will dry out.

## INKING THE STAMP

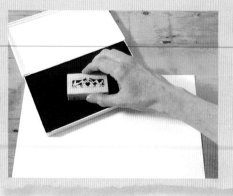

**1** Ink the stamp by tapping it *lightly* on the pad a couple of times. Avoid stamping hard into the pad or the stamp will be over-inked.

**2** Use a firm, even pressure to stamp. The larger the stamp, the more pressure will be needed to make a clear image.

**3** Always try out a motif by stamping on a scrap of paper first to make sure your stamp is evenly covered with ink – this avoids smudging or partially printed motifs.

## STAMPING WITH A MULTICOLORED INK PAD

**1** Ink the lower half of the stamp by tapping lightly on one half of the pad.

**2** Move the stamp and ink the upper half so the stamp is then covered in several different colors.

**3** Stamp a multicolored image. Alternatively, tap the stamp on the whole pad, without moving it, for a striped image. After three or four prints, wipe the colors gently off the pad with a tissue.

## APPLYING PAINT TO STAMPS

**1** Squeeze paint onto a plate or paint tray and, using a small roller, roll several times over the paint covering it evenly.

**2** Apply the paint by rolling back and forth once or twice over the stamp. Always try it out on a scrap of paper before printing to check that the coverage is even.

## APPLYING FELT-TIP PENS TO A STAMP

**1** Apply the felt tip directly to the stamp. Using fabric felt tips or pigment-based felt tips means you can apply several colors.

**2** Stamp while the ink is still wet.

## COLORING A STAMPED IMAGE

**1** Stamp onto your chosen surface and color in with art brush pens or fabric pens.

# HOW TO MAKE HOMEMADE STAMPS

*M*aking your own stamps is very satisfying and a few basic rules will ensure success. Keep your designs simple, cut them out clearly, and "get the feel" of applying paint and printing them, as they all vary slightly. Potatoes, sponge, and styrofoam can all be used very successfully to make homemade stamps.

### MATERIALS

\*

**Large potato**

\*

**Sharp kitchen knife**

\*

**Paper and pencil**

\*

**Scissors**

\*

**Craft knife**

\*

**Paint and large plate**

## MAKING A POTATO STAMP

**1** Cut a large potato in half with a sharp kitchen knife. A single chop will ensure the surface is even.

**2** Place the half you will use on a sheet of paper and draw around it with a pencil.

**3** Then you should draw a motif inside the exact shape of the potato half.

**4** Cut out the motif with scissors. This will give you a template for the potato design.

**TIP** To keep your potato for a few days, put it in a paper bag in the refrigerator. Keep the template or a tracing of the design so that if your stamp wears out before you have finished, you can make another.

**5** Place on the surface of the potato. The damp surface will keep it in place. Using a craft knife, cut the potato around the paper and scoop it out.

**6** To ink the potato stamp, spread an even coat of paint onto a large plate and dip the potato into the paint. Try it out on scrap paper before printing.

## MAKING A SPONGE STAMP

**1** Draw – or trace – a design on a piece of paper. Make sure it will fit your sponge.

**2** You should cut the design out carefully with scissors or a craft knife.

### MATERIALS

\*

**Paper and pencil**

\*

**Sponge**

\*

**Scissors or craft knife**

\*

**Repositioning glue**

\*

**Dark felt-tip pen**

\*

**Paint and large plate**

**3** Put a dab of repositioning glue on the design, place it on the sponge, and draw around it with a dark felt tip pen.

**4** Cut around the design with scissors or a craft knife.

**5** To print your sponge stamp, spread an even coat of paint onto a large plate and dab the sponge in the paint. Try it out on scrap paper before printing. Sponges are more absorbent than other stamps so more paint will be needed.

## MATERIALS

\*

**Paper and pencil**

\*

**Scissors or craft knife**

\*

**Styrofoam tile**

\*

**Dark felt-tip pen**

\*

**Medium-sized sewing needle**

\*

**Cork from a bottle**

\*

**Candle**

## MAKING A STYROFOAM STAMP

**1** Draw – or trace – a design onto paper. Cut out the design with scissors or a craft knife.

**2** Place the cutout design on the styrofoam tile and then draw around it carefully with a dark felt-tip pen.

**❸** Push a medium-sized sewing needle into a bottle cork with the sharp end out. Hold the tip of the needle over a lighted candle for about 6 seconds.

**❹** With the needle, cut around the outline in several stages. Practice first on a spare piece of styrofoam as the needle cuts very quickly. As the needle cools, it stops cutting, so it will have to be re-heated as you go.

# STAMP DESIGN AND EFFECTS

*When planning a design, stamp a number of motifs onto white paper, cut around them and arrange them on the item to be decorated. This enables you to try out different ideas before committing yourself. The many different effects that can be created depend on the type of stamp used, the ink or paint, and the surface.*

## PLANNING A DESIGN

For most projects, the simplest way of planning and spacing a design is to use paper cutouts. Stamp a number of the motifs you are using onto paper, making sure you print enough to give you a good idea how they should be placed. If you are using them for a wall or a slippery surface, use repositioning glue.

Arrange the cutout motifs on your project.

## HOMEMADE STAMP EFFECTS ON PAINTED WOODEN SURFACES

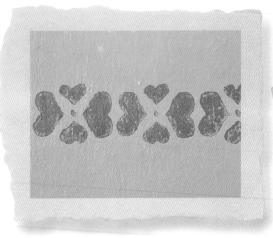

**1** Stamp made from an eraser (see page 8).

**2** Stamp made from a styrofoam tile.

**3** A stamp made from a potato is good for printing simple, bold shapes.

**4** Stamp made from an ordinary medium-density sponge.

## STAMPING WITH DIFFERENT PAINTS AND INKS

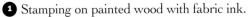

**1** Stamping on painted wood with fabric ink.

**2** Stamping on painted wood with acrylic paint creates an effect like this.

**③** Stamping on painted wood with white glue and gold metallic powder.

**④** Stamping on a fantasy finish with white glue and gold metallic powder.

## STAMPING ON FABRIC

**①** Stamping with fabric ink is very simple and straightforward. The ink dries almost immediately, does not require any special setting, and is non-toxic.

**②** Stamping with different-colored fabric pens applied directly to the stamp. Fabric pens have the same qualities as fabric ink, but with fabric paints you should always check manufacturers' instructions.

**③** Stamping with fabric paints.

# Stationery, Cards, & Gifts

# LETTERHEAD STATIONERY

MATERIALS

✳

**Stationery and**

**envelopes**

✳

**Ruler and pencil**

✳

**Stamps:** *tall Victorian*

*house and little*

*Victorian home*

✳

**Two art brush pens:**

*red, purple*

*Stationery with an address is infinitely useful. If you are starting your own business, letterhead is essential – and you can impress your clients with a simple classical motif. For personal letters, you may prefer to choose a stamp that echoes your temperament. You can also use special stamps for special occasions – hearts to a loved one, a tumbling clown to a favorite child, or a bouquet of flowers to a gardening friend.*

## CREATIVE STAMPING

Experiment with different colors and techniques. The same stamp can appear bold and primitive when primary colors are used, or elegant and sophisticated when embossed in gold (see opposite page).

**1** Measure the paper and mark the center about 1 in. (2.5cm) from the top of the paper.

**2** Using the red art brush pen, color directly onto the first stamp, the little Victorian home, and stamp immediately onto the center of the paper. Color the second motif, tall Victorian house, with the red pen as before and stamp on each side of the first motif.

**3** Using the purple art brush pen, add color only to the larger house in the center. By leaving the houses on each side as they are, the contrast gives the image more depth.

# EMBOSSED STATIONERY

MATERIALS

✳

**Stationery**

✳

**Ruler and pencil**

✳

**Little Victorian home**

**stamp**

✳

**Ink pad**

✳

**Gold embossing**

**powder**

✳

**Heat gun**

*$E$mbossing can be done either with an embossing pad and embossing ink or with colored pigment pads. In this case, I have used a pigment pad, but you should get the same attractive and glowing final result by using gold embossing powder.*

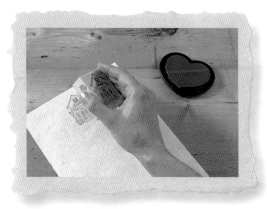

**1** Measure and mark the center of the paper, as on the opposite page. Press the Victorian home stamp onto the ink pad, then stamp it directly onto the stationery.

**Introduce a hint of glamour to your stationery – with embossed gold on elegant pale ivory paper.**

**2** Sprinkle gold embossing powder onto the wet image so that it is completely covered.

**3** Pour the excess powder onto a spare sheet of paper. (The powder can be used again.)

**4** Hold the heat gun over the gold-covered motif - the gold will melt almost immediately. If you use a different heat source, such as a toaster, it will take about 30 seconds. Embossing makes a stamp into a vibrant image.

# GIFT WRAP

*Stamps can create distinctive and stylish gift wrap in no time at all. You can design paper suitable for every imaginable occasion that no one will ever want to throw away — try paper embossed in silver and gold, tissue paper with harp-playing cherubs, or black musical notes on a shiny white background. Stamp beautiful handmade Mulberry paper and cover, or line, a favorite box. You can treat a battered book, treasured from childhood, in the same way. Stamp a suitable design onto Mulberry paper and make a cover, perhaps to show what it's about — a serious stamp for a serious subject, something frivolous for a potboiler. Try the unexpected, anything goes.*

## CREATIVE STAMPING

When stamping onto pale colored paper, pigment inks are suitable. However, when stamping onto darker shades of paper, acrylic paints give more contrast.

**1** Squeeze 2 in. (5cm) of yellow ocher, ultramarine blue, and white paint onto a plate.

**2** With a brush, mix the paints together until they have a smooth, creamy consistency.

**MATERIALS**

✳

**Mulberry paper in purple and green**

✳

**Acrylic paints:**

*yellow ocher,*

*ultramarine blue,*

*and white*

✳

**Paintbrush**

✳

**Oak leaf stamp**

✳

**Small roller and paint tray or plate**

**3** Transfer to a paint tray and roll the roller in them until it is evenly covered. (The paint can be left on the plate if there is no paint tray readily on hand.)

**4** Transfer the paint onto the stamp by rolling the roller over it once or twice for an even coverage.

**Stamp your own wrapping paper with a simple leaf design, stamped in blue on handmade Mulberry paper. Try it in other colors for a different effect.**

**5** Repeat the stamp at random on the Mulberry paper, making sure that they are fairly evenly spaced to avoid a muddled look. Re-ink each time you stamp.

# GIFT BAG

*Stamp your own gift bags for birthday presents, Christmas presents, or any special gift. This one has been embossed for extra sparkle.*

MATERIALS

*

**Gift bag**

*

**Stamp design of your choice (diamond center quilt stamp is used here)**

*

**Embossing pad or pigment pad**

*

**Mulberry paper (pink or white)**

*

**Gold embossing powder**

*

**Spare sheet of paper**

*

**Heat gun**

*

**Art brush pens:** *blue, red, mauve, purple*

*

**Scissors**

*

**Glue**

**1** Press the stamp on the embossing or pigment pad in order to ink it.

**2** Press the stamp firmly onto the pink or white mulberry paper.

**3** While the ink is still wet, sprinkle gold embossing powder over the entire image. The powder will stick to the wet ink. Shake off the excess powder onto spare paper – it can later be returned to the jar and reused.

**4** Hold the heat gun over the powder-covered image until the powder melts into a glowing gold.

**5** Using art brush pens, color in the stamped image.

**6** Cut out and glue each of the embossed stamp designs into place onto the gift bag.

**An eye-catching gift bag in vibrant colors for that special gift.**

# PENGUIN GREETING CARD

*A*nimals and birds - like these splendid penguins - make perfect subjects for cards. Simple and stylish, they are equally suitable for adults and children and will delight all who receive them.

## MATERIALS
❋
**White mulberry paper**
❋
**Deckle-edge scissors**
❋
**Beige blank card and envelope**
❋
**Penguin stamp**
❋
**Onyx pigment stamp pad**
❋
**Piece of white paper**
❋
**Black art brush pen**
❋
**Glue**

**1** Cut out a piece of the white mulberry paper (handmade paper), slightly smaller than the card, with the deckle-edge scissors.

**2** Ink the penguin stamp with the onyx pigment pad. First, stamp onto a piece of scrap paper to ensure even coverage.

**3** Stamp four penguins onto mulberry paper. Print the two penguins at the top first, and then print the two underneath. Re-ink the stamp each time.

**4** With the deckle-edge scissors, cut out a piece of white paper slightly larger than the mulberry paper, allowing a 1¼-in. (3-cm) border all the way around. Using a black art brush pen, fill in the border.

**5** Glue the penguin images onto the white paper with black border.

**6** Spread the glue evenly onto the back of the white paper. Position carefully onto the blank card and glue into place.

**Penguins stamped with eye-catching simplicity create a card suitable for any event.**

# SUNFLOWER GREETING CARD

*C*elebrate Christmas, birthdays, or any special occasion by stamping your own unique cards. There are beautiful handmade blank cards available, made from recycled paper. Here I have used attractive red mulberry paper and a sunflower stamp as the basis of the card design. Embossing the sunflower head gives it that extra sparkle.

**1** Follow steps 1–6 for the Gift Bag on pages 28–9. The same procedure is used here to emboss the stamped design. This produces a lovely, glittering image.

## MATERIALS

✳

**Large flower stamp (a sunflower design is used here)**

✳

**Embossing pad and ink**

✳

**1 piece of white cartridge paper**

✳

**Gold embossing powder**

✳

**Heat gun**

✳

**Art brush pens:**

*yellow, orange, red*

✳

**Craft knife**

✳

**Cutting mat or sheet of glass with taped edges**

✳

**Red mulberry paper**

✳

**Handmade blank card and envelope**

✳

**Glue**

**2** Place the sunflower on a cutting mat. With a craft knife, you should carefully cut out the bright sunflower head, as shown in the photograph above.

**3** Carefully tear a small rectangular piece of red mulberry paper – handmade mulberry paper looks most attractive when torn, with rough, rather feathery edges.

**4** Glue the mulberry paper onto the left-hand side of the blank card.

**5** Position the flower head in the center of the card, overlapping the mulberry paper, and glue into place.

Brighten the gloomiest day with a bright and jolly sunflower stamp. This pretty design is then embossed with gold powder for a special, glittering effect.

# FILE

**MATERIALS**

✳

**1 dark blue file**

✳

**2 handmade stamps**

**of a sun and stars**

**(see Templates)**

✳

**Gold acrylic paint**

✳

**Small roller and paint**

**tray or plate**

*Stamps provide a perfect opportunity to decorate your files and perhaps even help in sorting out all those dreary bits of paper that so often, in my experience, get mislaid at the bottom of the wrong box. Files and box files can be stamped with different motifs, according to their use, for immediate identification – vegetables and herbs for recipes, flowers for gardening, more formal images for bills and receipts, and a jolly motif for letters awaiting an answer. Stamp files to match the colors in a room or, using the same motif, stamp files in various colors for each member of the family – and encourage their organizational skills! I have used two handmade stamps, cut from rubber-backed felt and an eraser.*

### CREATIVE STAMPING

Even if you have a good eye, it is a good idea to measure and plan out before you start to stamp. A simple way of measuring for a file is to cut a piece of paper the same size as the back (or front), fold the length in half, then in half again to make four sections. Do the same with the width of the paper, fold in half twice, making 16 sections altogether. Pierce a small hole in the paper and, placing the paper over the front and back of the file, make a small dot with a gold felt tip. This will be covered up by the gold sun.

**1** Apply gold acrylic paint to the sun stamp using the small roller.

**2** Stamp firmly onto the file over the gold mark. Place your free hand inside the file under the stamp to provide even pressure.

**3** Apply gold acrylic paint to the stars stamp and print between the suns.

**4** Using the roller and gold acrylic paint, carefully apply paint around the edge.

**Golden suns and stars transform this ordinary blue file into something special.**

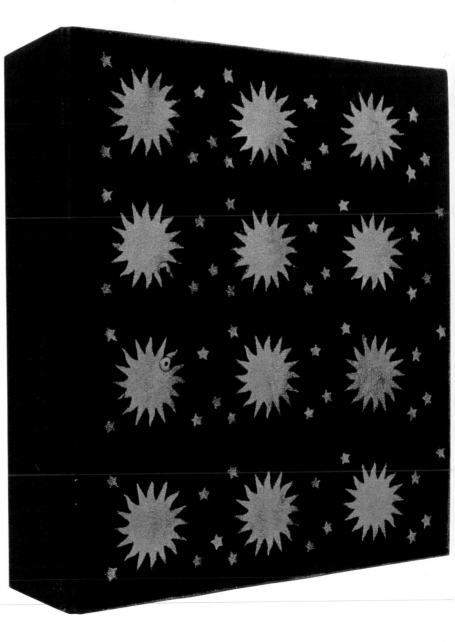

*Stamping is ideal for paper – you can use it for sumptuous stationery or pretty gift wrap. Your friends will be delighted with a present wrapped in such a stylish way. Use stamping, too, for bags and decorative boxes.*

*Dinner by candlelight is so romantic! These church candles are stamped with suns and ladybugs and will add glamour to any dining table. For a gardening friend, why not give stamped terracotta pots like these to add interest to a patio?*

# CANDLES

MATERIALS

❋

**Large altar candle**

❋

**Acrylic paints:**

*phthalo blue, ivory*

*black, antique gold*

❋

**Small roller and**

**paint tray or plate**

❋

**Palette knife**

❋

**Stamps:** *primitive sun*

*and star cluster*

❋

**Mineral spirits**

❋

**Soft rags**

*Candlelight creates the most subtle and magical atmosphere, bringing out the romantic in us all. You can stamp a candle just for that special occasion. Alternatively, an arrangement of several large candles beautifully stamped makes an original and focal point in any room — without even lighting them!*

**TIP** Acrylic paints or fabric inks are both suitable for stamping on candles. Stamping onto a rounded surface is a delicate operation and needs care. The trick is to begin at one edge of the stamp and, with a steady hand, roll from right to left (left to right if you are left-handed). A slight slip, with this motif, almost adds to its appeal.

**1** Squeeze 2in. (5cm) of phthalo blue and ivory black onto a paint tray or plate and mix thoroughly with a palette knife.

**3** Squeeze 2in. (5cm) of gold acrylic paint on to a paint tray or plate and apply to the star cluster stamp.

**2** With a small roller, apply the dark blue paint to the primitive sun stamp, insuring that the paint is evenly distributed over the stamp. Stamp up and down the candle, reapplying the dark blue paint each time.

**Spectacular candles stamped in dark blue and gold.**

**4** Stamp stars in the center of all the suns, reapplying paint for each motif.

# CRACKLEGLAZE BOX

*Crackleglaze is great fun to do and can be applied to a variety of different objects. First efforts, however, are best applied to something small and simple, without adornment or too many round edges. Once proficient, you can branch out and be more daring. The important thing is not to be put off if those first attempts look less than professional. It can be very disappointing – when you are anticipating the second coat gently cracking to reveal the first coat underneath – to be faced with pools of paint in one corner and bare patches in another. Practice first on spare pieces of wood. The trick is to get both the paint consistency and the pressure of the paint-brush just right. You will soon be addicted to your new skill.*

## PAINTBOX

Crackleglaze varnish is a water-based glaze which, when applied between two coats of water-based paints of contrasting colors, causes them to separate. Any water-based paint will work. In this instance I have used acrylic with a tiny amount of latex to give it body. Latex alone will work equally well, but I used acrylic to mix the exact colors that I wanted to use.

**1** For the first coat, mix together 3in. (7.5cm) of Venetian red with 1in. (2.5cm) of yellow ocher and ¼in. (6mm) of cadmium. Add a drop of water and about a tablespoon of latex paint and mix to a smooth consistency. The latex gives the mixture body. If the color is too pale, add more acrylic paint. Apply, keeping the brush strokes in the same direction. Leave until it is completely dry.

**2** Apply the crackleglaze varnish with a clean dry brush. Keep the brushstrokes in the same direction as before. Leave until it is completely dry.

**3** For the second coat, mix together 3in. (7.5cm) of cobalt blue and 1in. (2.5cm) each of yellow ocher and raw umber. Add white latex paint – about two tablespoonfuls – and mix to a smooth consistency. Apply the second coat of paint, brushing in the opposite direction to the glaze and the first coat of paint. Keep the brush fairly heavily loaded but not so much that the paint drops off. Brush evenly in one continuous stroke and *do not* paint over the same area twice. Leave to dry.

**4** Ink the stamp for the central motif using the fabric ink pad with blue and brown fabric paint worked into it. (These colors produce an "old" look in keeping with the final "antique" look of the box.) Stamp onto a piece of paper.

**5** Using a cutting mat and a craft knife, carefully cut out the central motif.

**6** Glue onto the center of the box. Press the motif down firmly.

**7** Using a small roller, apply Venetian red paint to the border stamp and apply the design around the edge of the box lid.

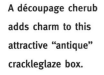 **9** Apply one coat of French polish to prevent the gold from dissolving. Then apply four coats of clear matte varnish, sanding between each application. When the final coat is dry, apply furniture polish and buff to a rich shine.

If you want to create an aged look, add a tiny amount of raw umber artist's oil paint to the final two coats of varnish.

**8** Using the gold marker pen, draw a line around the top edge of the box.

**A découpage cherub adds charm to this attractive "antique" crackleglaze box.**

# TERRACOTTA POTS

*My first trip to Andalucia in Spain was remarkable among other things for the wealth of photographs I brought back of doorways, windows, balconies, walls, and every little nook and cranny crammed with colorful terracotta pots. Once home, I painted every terracotta pot I could lay my hands on. Now, with the advent of stamping, I can begin again. There is no need to buy new ones — old ones look just as good and are fun to do.*

### PAINTBOX

Acrylic paints are ideal for painting and stamping on terracotta pots. The large range of colors gives an excellent choice for experimentation. They dry quickly and are washable. Clean your brushes and stamps in warm, soapy water before the paint dries.

**1** Stamp a number of folk basket motifs onto white paper. Cut around them and, using repositioning glue, arrange them around the rim. Make a small mark underneath each motif to use as a guide to stamping.

### MATERIALS

\*

**2 terracotta pots**

\*

**Stamps:** *floral and folk basket*

\*

**White paper**

\*

**Scissors**

\*

**Repositioning glue**

\*

**Acrylic paints:** *phthalo blue, burnt umber, yellow ocher, cadmium yellow, white*

\*

**Palette knife**

\*

**Paintbrushes**

\*

**Small roller and paint tray or plate**

These brightly decorated terracotta pots would look equally impressive massed together indoors or outside.

**2** Squeeze 3in. (7.5cm) of phthalo blue onto a paint tray or plate, with 2in. (5cm) of burnt umber and 1in. (2.5cm) of white. Mix well with a palette knife.

Mix 3in. (7.5cm) of yellow ocher in a paint tray or plate with 1in. (2.5cm) each of cadmium yellow and white.

**3** Paint one terracotta pot with two coats of the blue paint. Leave it to dry before applying the second coat. Apply two coats of yellow paint to the other pot. Leave to dry between coats. Paint the second coat roughly for a more rustic look.

**4** Apply yellow paint to the floral stamp with a small roller, insuring the stamp is well covered. Try it out on a spare piece of paper first. Keep a piece of damp rag handy to wipe off any mistakes.

**5** Hold the pot firmly with one hand and stamp the floral motif carefully onto the blue terracotta pot, rolling it slightly from right to left (or left to right if you are left-handed).

**6** Apply yellow paint to the folk basket stamp with a small roller, again trying out on a spare piece of paper first.

**7** Stamp around the rim of the pot.

Repeat stages 4, 5, 6, and 7, using the blue paint to stamp the same motifs onto the yellow pot.

# YELLOW LACQUER BOX

Negoro nuri *was a lovely form of lacquering developed in the fourteenth century by Japanese monks, who often used it to decorate simple bowls for their meals. Traditionally, it consisted of lacquering first in black and then in red with parts of the red rubbed away to reveal the patches of black beneath. One variation substituted a yellow lacquer instead of red over the black, and sometimes grains of rice were pressed into the still sticky black base, to be removed when dry. So when the article was completed, the tiny depressions left by the rice were revealed. The technique of lacquering was a long slow process of many layers, and the finished result was a flawless glowing surface, impervious to scratches. However, there are simpler and quicker ways of achieving this beautiful finish. And, instead of adding decoration when the object was finished by incising a pattern to reveal the color beneath, you can stamp on a motif in black. In this case, I have, in fact, added the decorative motif before finishing the lacquering so that it becomes an integral part of the design. It is advisable to begin with something simple like this small box.*

## PAINTBOX

Acrylic paints are suitable for this project. However, the first base coats of black should be painted using flat oil paint as it is more durable when rubbing through.

**1** Paint the box with two coats of flat black oil paint. Allow to dry thoroughly between coats and sand lightly.

When completely dry, rub an ordinary household candle unevenly over the surface of the box.

**2** Squeeze 4in. (10cm) each of chrome yellow and raw sienna onto a plate and mix thoroughly with a palette knife. You will need to mix this amount for each coat each time or it will dry out on the plate. Apply four coats with the soft-haired paintbrush. Leave to dry between coats and sand lightly.

## MATERIALS

✳

**Small wooden box**

✳

**Small bristle paintbrush**

✳

**Small can of flat black oil paint**

✳

**Fine-grade wet and dry sandpaper (600)**

✳

**Candle**

✳

**Acrylic paints:** *chrome yellow, raw sienna, black*

✳

**Palette knife**

✳

**Soft-haired paintbrush, sable or synthetic, size 6**

✳

**Medium-grade steel wool**

✳

**Orchid stamp**

✳

**Black fabric ink and pad**

✳

**White paper**

✳

**French polish**

✳

**Denatured alcohol**

✳

**Mineral spirits**

✳

**Soft lint-free cloth**

**3** When completely dry, use medium-grade steel wool to rub patches in the yellow surface. The aim is to reveal a few small areas of the black undercoat, imitating actual wear and tear. Rub over the surface with fine-grade wet and dry sandpaper.

**4** Ink the orchid stamp with black fabric ink. Try it out on a piece of paper to check the effect first.

**TIP** Applying French polish requires accuracy, speed, deftness, and skill, so it is a good idea to practice first on a piece of painted wood. Work in a warm, dry atmosphere using quick, even strokes. Do not go over the same area twice. And don't give up – it's worth the effort!

**5** Stamp on one end of the box, pressing firmly and evenly. Re-ink and stamp the other end of the box in the same way.

**6** Pour equal amounts of French polish and denatured alcohol into a container. Dip into the mixture a soft lint-free cloth and wipe over the surface of the box, one side at a time, taking care not to handle the wet areas. Leave to dry for an hour before applying the next coat. Apply six to ten coats or more if you have the patience, sanding between each one with wet fine-grade wet and dry sandpaper.

**A striking effect is produced by layers of French polish over a distressed yellow base.**

# Fabrics & Clothes

# TABLECLOTH AND NAPKINS

*W*ith stamps, you can create tablecloths for all occasions – special ones for Christmas and birthdays, or an attractive variety of designs simply for different meals. Something bright and jolly cheers up those bleak winter mornings at breakfast, while something simple and elegant is more appropriate for entertaining, and a pretty stamped design is appealing for everyday use.

## MATERIALS

✳

**Circular tablecloth with scalloped edges**

✳

**Napkins**

✳

**Fabric paints:**

*green, yellow, blue, purple, red*

✳

**Large vine leaf and grapes stamps, or other stamps of your choice**

✳

**Three small rollers**

✳

**Three bowls or plates**

### PAINTBOX

Various different paints are available for use on fabric, and most of them can be used for stamping. Avoid the very runny ones. While these are suitable for painting directly onto fabric, they don't work on stamps.

Instructions vary, so it is important always to check the manufacturer's directions. Some paints, for instance, require ironing to set them, while others can be simply left to dry. There are some types of acrylic paints which, when mixed with a fabric medium, can be used for stamping. Fabric ink on an ink pad is suitable for stamping on delicate materials and paler colors, but on heavier and darker fabrics it will not show up.

**❶** To obtain the effect created here, you need to mix the fabric paints in three different containers. In one bowl, mix green with a small amount of blue. In the second bowl, mix green with a small amount of yellow and red. In the third bowl, mix the purple with a small amount of yellow paint.

**T I P** Before printing on new fabric, it should be washed to remove the sizing. When it is dry, iron and place on a hard smooth surface to work. You will need to tape it into place to prevent it from slipping. For an even print, stamping on fabric requires more pressure than on other surfaces.

**❷** Apply the green/blue fabric paint and the green/yellow/red fabric paint to the vine leaf stamp. Do this using two rollers coated in the two different colors. First roll the green/blue onto half the stamp and then roll on the green/yellow/red. There is no need to be exact – if the two colors merge, it looks more attractive. Stamp around the scalloped edge.

**3** Apply all three mixed colors to the large grapes stamp. Roll the blue/green and green/yellow/red fabric paint onto the leaves and the purple paint onto the grapes. Again there is no need to be too exact; just allow the colors to blend.

**4** Stamp onto the tablecloth at regular intervals. Unless you have a good eye, it is wise to measure to plan where you place the motifs. Totally random is one thing, cockeyed is quite another.

**5** For the napkins, prepare the fabric in the same way as the tablecloth.

Apply green/blue, green/yellow/red and purple fabric paint to the large grape stamp as before and stamp the motif at each corner of the napkins.

**Bunches of grapes and vine leaves create a beautiful tablecloth.**

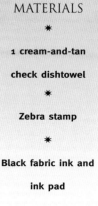

# DISHTOWELS

**MATERIALS**

\*

**1 cream-and-tan**

**check dishtowel**

\*

**Zebra stamp**

\*

**Black fabric ink and**

**ink pad**

*D*ishtowels nowadays come in every imaginable color and design, from souvenirs of trips abroad to your astrological star sign. There's no reason, however, why you should not stamp your own for a set that is quite unique to you. A set of themed dishtowels would make a good present, too.

## PAINTBOX

There are various different paints and inks available for printing onto fabrics, and most of these can be used for stamping. For this dishtowel, I have used fabric ink on an ink pad which is a suitable method for this particular image, black on cream. Always check the manufacturer's instructions when using fabric paints. Some fabric inks do not need any special setting, and, once dry, they are washable. *Always wash new fabric before printing to remove the sizing.*

**TIP** Mistakes cannot be rectified when stamping onto fabric, so it is a good idea to practice first on scraps of material similar to the one you are printing on.

**1** Pour black fabric ink onto the ink pad and massage it well into the pad.

**2** Ink the stamp by tapping it several times on the pad. Turn the stamp over and look at the rubber to check it has enough ink.

**Handsome zebras stamped onto dishtowels bring a touch of stylish fun to the kitchen.**

**3** Place the dishtowel on a hard, even surface and press the stamp firmly onto the material. Re-ink the stamp for each repetition.

# HAND TOWEL

## MATERIALS

✳

**Hand towel**

✳

**Dark blue satin rib-
bon, twice the width
of the towel plus
6in. (15cm) extra**

✳

**Acrylic fabric paint:**

*golden ocher, white*

✳

**Acrylic fabric medium**

✳

**Shell stamp**

✳

**Sewing materials,
needle, thread, and
scissors/sewing
machine**

*S*tamping on terrycloth may seem impossible, but in fact there is a simple way around the problem. Stamp on ribbon and sew it on. This has distinct advantages – if you tire of your print or change your bathroom decor, simply print a brand-new design. Different colored ribbons for different members of the family might just encourage them to stick to their own! Children could also choose their own stamp – or could make one.

### PAINTBOX

Any fabric paints would be suitable to print on this dark blue ribbon. I have used acrylic fabric paints with a fabric medium. Fabric inks are *not* appropriate to print on dark colors. Always read the manufacturer's instructions to check whether or not ironing is needed to set the image.

**1** Wash and iron the ribbon to remove the dressing. Cut the ribbon to size leaving ½in. (1.3cm) at each end to turn under. Spread out on an even, firm surface.

**2** Squeeze out 3in. (7.5cm) of golden ocher paint onto a paint tray or plate. Add ½in. (1.3cm) of white and mix well with palette knife. Add 1 tsp. of fabric medium and blend in thoroughly.

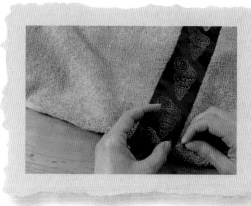

**3** Apply the yellow fabric paint to the shell stamp, insuring it is well covered. Practice on a piece of spare ribbon first, then stamp onto the ribbon itself. Reapply paint for each motif and continue printing to the end of the ribbon.

**4** When dry, sew the ribbon onto both ends of the towel.

**A towel stamped with
seashells on contrasting
blue satin.**

# BED LINENS

MATERIALS

\*

Sheets and

pillowcases

\*

Fabric inks: *black and*

*blue*

\*

Ink pad

\*

Two stamps, in the

designs of your

choice (humming

bird and butterfly

designs were used

here)

\*

Blue fabric crayon

\*

Lace

\*

Needle and thread or

sewing machine

*Bed linens nowadays come in every imaginable color and design, often to match curtains and wallpaper. Perhaps this is even more reason to create one's own personalized linen – an individual motif that holds some special meaning or maybe ornate initials like those grand old monogrammed sheets. Beautiful old Toille de Jouy (an eighteenth-century country print, using copper plate) was my inspiration for the border on these sheets and pillowcases.*

### PAINTBOX

As I was stamping onto white and wanted a fine clear image, I used fabric ink on an ink pad. These come in a variety of clear, bright colors which can be mixed on the pad by pouring each ink on separately and massaging in. Fabric crayons or fabric felt tips can be used to add more color to the image; in this case, a fabric crayon was used.

**1** If your bed linens are new, wash them first to remove the sizing. Iron and place on smooth hard surface.

To create a color nearer to the original Toille than the blue on its own, mix together the two fabric inks. Pour the blue and the black onto the ink pad until it is well covered. Massage well into the pad.

**2** Press the first stamp onto the ink pad so it is well inked and stamp onto the sheet, pressing down firmly. More pressure is needed when stamping on fabric than paper or wood.

**T I P** Practice stamping on spare pieces of fabric before you begin. Mistakes *cannot* be removed.

**3** Ink the second stamp well and stamp next to the first motif. Continue to the end of the border, alternating the two images.

**4** Using pale blue fabric crayon, enhance the shaded areas on the images.

**5** Sew lace along the border of the sheets, using a needle and thread or sewing machine.

For the pillowcase, repeat, using the same method as for the sheets. Stamp the two images at opposite corners.

Crisp, white, lace-trimmed sheets and matching pillowcases, stamped with birds and butterflies.

# GAUZE CURTAINS

### MATERIALS
*
**White gauze**
*
**Cherub and Small
Sun stamps**
*
**Gold fabric paint**
*
**Small roller and
paint tray or plate**

*Billowing, floating gauze adds style to the plainest of windows and stamping enhances this pretty material even more. The special quality of gauze is the way it drapes so beautifully, producing a sense of the exotic. The delightful harp-playing cherub stamped here in gold looks wonderful floating alongside a simple sun. Why not stamp some more fabric and drape it around the bed?*

**1** Apply gold paint to the Cherub stamp, using a small roller. Stamp first on a piece of scrap paper to make sure it is well covered.

### PAINTBOX

There are a number of gold fabric paints available, and the colors can vary considerably – some are more brown than gold. The one used here is an Antique Gold acrylic mixed with a fabric medium. Acrylic paints, in particular, dry quickly. Always check the manufacturer's instructions, as some paints require ironing to set them, while others can simply be left to dry. Whatever paints are used, when printing numerous images clean the stamp regularly with stamp cleaner to keep the image crisp and to prevent the stamp from clogging.

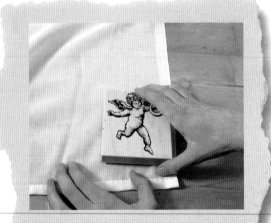

**2** Stamp onto the gauze, using a firm, even pressure. Re-ink the stamp for each motif. Stamp eight motifs, then clean the stamp in order to maintain a clear image.

**❸** Apply gold paint to the Small Sun motif in the same way and press firmly onto the fabric. Re-ink the stamp for each motif. Clean the stamp after stamping twelve motifs.

**TIP** Cut the gauze to fit your windows, allowing for hemming top and bottom. Print the fabric before you sew the curtains. If possible, use a table large enough to spread the width of the material out flat. Support the length of the fabric with a couple of chairs or a bench so that it doesn't drag on the floor. With such a fine fabric, it is useful to place a large sheet of white paper under the gauze. A simple way of measuring the distance between each print is to use the span of your hand. Stamp the first cherub at the bottom right-hand corner (left-hand if you are left-handed), spread your hand with the little finger at the head of the cherub, and stamp the sun where your thumb rests. Continue along the lower edge and do the same for the next row.

**A touch of the exotic – gossamer-fine gauze curtains stamped in glittering gold.**

# PILLOWS

MATERIALS

✳

**Pillow cover**

✳

**Stamps:** *folk art urn*
*with flowers and small*
*folk art basket*

✳

**Several sheets of**
**white paper**

✳

**Scissors**

✳

**Small roller and**
**paint tray or plate**

✳

**Jar of dark blue**
**fabric paint**

*If you want to give a room a total revamp, nothing could be simpler than stamping some cheery, bright pillows and scattering them around the room. Use contrasting colors or blend with the existing color scheme. If you have a particular design you like on your curtains or other upholstery fabric, this is a good opportunity to make a stamp of your own to coordinate with it. The motifs need not all be the same, though. Alternatively, print a matching motif in different colors. You can print a different stamp, though of a similar theme, to ensure harmony. This pillow is printed on raw silk. You can stamp on most materials, but avoid some of the heavier upholstery fabrics as they are not suitable. Whatever you do, you will be creating your own unique pillows.*

## PAINTBOX

Fabric paint is widely available in art and craft stores and ideal for stamping on pillows. Make sure you purchase fabric paint for printing and *not* for painting, as the latter is runny and not suitable for stamping. Always read the manufacturer's instructions to check whether or not ironing is needed to set your print.

**1** If it is new, wash and iron the pillow cover to remove the sizing.

To plan your design, stamp a number of the two motifs (the more the better) on white paper, cut them out, and arrange them on the pillow until you are satisfied with the design, remove them one at a time and, with the cover on a firm even surface, stamp in its place.

**2** Apply paint to the folk art flower stamp, using a small roller and blue fabric paint. Make sure the paint is evenly distributed.

**3** Remove the first cut-out motif and stamp firmly onto the pillow cover. Continue to stamp all the folk flower motifs, re-applying fabric paint for each motif. When you have stamped six motifs, clean the stamp with stamp cleaner to maintain a clear image.

**4** Apply dark blue fabric paint to the small folk basket stamp, using the small roller. With such a small stamp, it is important not to overload it with paint. Stamp first on a scrap of spare material to check this.

This distinctive pillow stamped in dark blue on rich yellow silk is both stylish and colorful.

**5** Removing the paper cutout motifs, one at a time, stamp firmly onto the cover between the folk flower motifs. Continue until you have stamped in place all of the cutouts, reapplying fabric paint for each motif, and cleaning the stamp with stamp cleaner after six motifs to maintain a clear image.

*Fabrics, whether clothes or household items, can be stamped with the various fabric paints available. Use stamping for table linen, a stylish shade, or for cheerful kitchen apparel. Stamping is also suitable for walls — these pineapples and radishes would make any kitchen look jolly.*

*You can make a lovely bedroom by using stamps to enhance and coordinate. Here, the bedlinen, headboard, and bedroom wall are all stamped — you can stamp directly on a wall or use paper cutouts. Delicate organdy curtains look especially pretty when stamped.*

# WINDOW SHADE

## MATERIALS

*

**Ivory shade**

*

**Acrylic fabric paint:**

*phthalo blue, yellow*

*ocher, raw umber,*

*white*

*

**Paint tray or plate**

*

**Palette knife**

*

**Acrylic fabric medium**

*

**Ivy leaf stamp**

*

**White paper**

*

**Scissors**

*

**Pencil**

*

**Small roller**

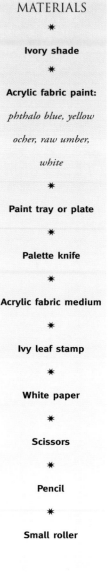

*Stamping your own shade means that you will be able to match exactly your curtains or wallpaper. If you can't find a manufactured stamp, make your own. This beautiful ivy leaf stamp is both simple and attractive, stamped along the edge of the shade.*

## PAINTBOX

For this shade, I used acrylic fabric paints with acrylic fabric medium because I wanted to achieve a particular faded blue. Acrylic fabric paints have a great choice of colors with which to experiment.

**1** Squeeze 3in. (7.5cm) of phthalo blue onto a paint tray or plate with 2in. (5cm) of raw umber and 1in. (2.5cm) each of yellow ocher and white. Mix well with a palette knife. Add 2 tsp. of fabric medium and again mix well with a palette knife.

**2** Stamp a number of ivy leaf motifs on a piece of white paper, then cut around them and arrange them along the edge of the shade until you are satisfied with their positioning and spacing. Then you should make a small mark, using a soft pencil as a guide.

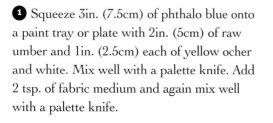

**3** With the small roller, apply fabric paint to the ivy leaf stamp, insuring it is well covered. Before printing onto the shade, try it out first on a scrap of similar fabric.

**4** Place the shade on a firm even surface and, following your guide marks, print onto the shade applying a firm, even pressure. Reapply paint for each motif. After four prints, clean the stamp with stamp cleaner to maintain a clear image.

For a really individual
look, stamp a plain
shade with motifs to
match your decor.

# SILK CAMISOLE

MATERIALS

✳

**Silk camisole**

✳

**Tracing paper**

✳

**Soft pencil**

✳

**2 pieces of white typing paper**

✳

**Fabric pens:**
*yellow and red*

✳

**Daisy stamp**

✳

**Scissors**

✳

**Repositioning glue**

*W*hat could be more luxurious than a drawer full of hand-printed silk underwear? Create something bright and frivolous, subtle and sophisticated, or pretty and alluring to suit the mood of the day. A silk camisole would also make a beautiful gift, personalized with, for instance, the recipient's favorite flower. The pretty daisy design on this camisole has been stamped around the neck, but it would look equally attractive stamped over the entire garment.

**1** Place the camisole on a flat, even surface, trace the neckline and armholes, and transfer to a piece of white paper. Apply ink to the stamp with the pens and stamp six daisies onto the second piece of paper. Cut around them with scissors – there is no need to be too exact – and arrange them symmetrically on the tracing of the camisole, two complete daisies on each side of the neck and three daisy heads along the front. Anchor them in place with repositioning glue to use as a guide when you start printing.

**2** Apply a yellow fabric pen to the center of the daisy, coloring straight onto the rubber stamp. Apply the red fabric pen, immediately, to the rest of the daisy. Print first onto a piece of scrap paper to insure even coverage.

**PAINTBOX**

Art brush pens for fabric are perfect for stamping onto this fine cream silk. Apply them directly onto the stamp to pick out details in different colors on specific areas. The daisy design used here has a different colored center from the rest of the flower. Fabric pens are fast and washable once dry.

❸ Place the camisole on a firm, even surface and stamp the daisy onto it. When the complete daisies have been stamped on each side of the neck, clean the stamp *very* carefully removing all the ink – try it out on a piece of paper first to check the rest of the stamp is clean. Ink just the daisy head and stamp three heads along the front of the neckline.

**The finished camisole with its pretty daisy-chain stamped around the neckline.**

# PAJAMAS

MATERIALS

*

Cotton pajamas

*

Two different
butterfly stamps

*

Fabric pens:

*red, yellow, and lilac*

*These gossamer-fine pajamas deserve an equally fine and delicate design. Flowers seemed too obvious, whereas butterflies with their ethereal delicacy were perfect – the translucency of the fabric adding to the beauty of the print. Stamp them as a gift or, using the same motifs, give a new lease on life and luxury to a favorite pair of your own pajamas.*

## PAINTBOX

Art brush pens for fabric are ideal for pale-colored, delicate fabrics, and they are very simple to use. They are particularly useful when using several different colors on a detailed stamp. You should choose your colors carefully. Test on a separate piece of fabric to see how they blend together, aiming for subtle and faded colors. Once dry, they are completely fast and washable.

**1** If you are using new fabric, wash it first to remove the sizing.

**2** Stamp a number of butterfly motifs on a clean sheet of paper. Cut around them and arrange them on the front of the pajamas until you have achieved a satisfactory and pleasing design. These will be your guide for printing.

**3** Using the yellow pen, ink the butterfly stamp completely. Here, I have used the "Swallowtail" stamp.

**4** Apply lilac to the center of the same stamp, allowing the color to spread a little so the edges are not too straight.

**5** Apply the red pen to the edges, allowing it to merge with the lilac.

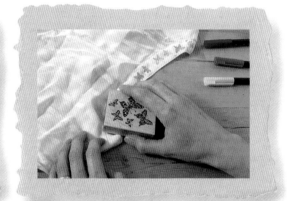

**Clusters of butterflies bring a touch of elegance to these silk pajamas.**

**6** Place pajamas on a firm, even surface. Put a clean sheet of white paper inside the pajamas. Stamp firmly onto the material. Re-ink the stamp for each print.

**7** Repeat steps 3–5 on the other stamp. Here I have used "Butterfly Medley." Color just three of the small butterflies to fit on the narrow neckband. Stamp firmly onto the neckband and repeat all the way around, re-inking stamp for each print.

# ROBE

## MATERIALS

\*

**Cream cotton jersey**

**robe with belt**

\*

**Fabric inks:**

*red, yellow, and purple*

\*

**3 ink pads**

\*

**Butterfly stamp**

*You can use stamping to team up different garments so they form a set. Here I have stamped the same pretty butterflies onto the wide collar and the belt of the robe to match the pajamas. This lovely, stylish bedtime apparel will give you a feeling of glamour – or make an appealing gift for a relative or friend.*

PAINTBOX

The material for the robe is heavier than that of the pajamas, so fabric pens would not be suitable. Instead, I have used fabric inks on ink pads in the same colors.

**1** Wash the robe to remove the sizing and iron flat.

**2** Apply purple ink to one half of the ink pad and rub in until it is well covered. Apply yellow ink to the other half of the pad and red ink to the other ink pad in the same way.

**3** Ink the stamp by pressing it firmly onto the ink pad, half of it onto the yellow and half onto the purple.

**4** Apply the edges of the stamp onto the red ink pad – in this way the butterflies will print in several different colors. Re-ink the stamp for each print. If the colors begin to look muddy, clean the stamp, apply more ink to the pads, and continue.

**Match the pajamas with this stylish robe, also stamped with butterflies.**

**5** Place the robe on a firm, even surface and then stamp the butterflies onto the collar.

**6** Ink the butterfly stamp with the same three colors and print onto the robe's belt.

# APRON AND CHEF'S HAT

*These wonderful fruit and vegetable stamps could be stamped on all kinds of things in the kitchen from tiles to files, even the walls or the seats and backs of plain wooden chairs. A simple muslin apron is a good place to start. Stamp as many or as few motifs as you like, and paint them in cheerful bright colors. To match the apron and cut a bit of a dash, why not use the same motifs and stamp a chef's hat?*

## PAINTBOX

Fabric ink on a pad is a quick and easy way of stamping these motifs. It is also particularly appropriate where a motif is to be filled in later with fabric paint, as it dries quickly and needs no ironing to make it fast. Mistakes on fabric can't be rectified, so it is advisable to practice printing on scraps of similar material first to gauge the amount of ink and pressure needed to make a clear print. Fabric paints, however, do need ironing to set the image. But they are simple to apply, the colors blend well, and they can be made darker by painting several coats or paler by adding a little water. Read the manufacturer's instructions to check whether or not the fabric paint you use needs ironing to set.

**1** Wash and iron the apron to remove the sizing.

**2** Apply black fabric ink to the ink pad and massage in well.

MATERIALS

✳

A muslin apron

✳

A chef's hat

✳

Black fabric ink and ink pad

✳

Fruit and vegetable stamps: *corn, radishes, pineapple, artichoke*

✳

Fabric paints: *red, yellow, green*

✳

Containers for paints – palette or bowls

✳

Jar of water

✳

Sable paintbrush, size 4

**3** Ink the pineapple stamp with black ink. Check that it is well covered. Place the apron on a firm, even surface and stamp it.

**❼** To decorate the chef's hat, repeat the steps as for the apron. Arrange the stamps randomly around the rim.

**A chef's hat with stamped and painted motifs to match the apron.**

**❹** Ink the radish stamp with black ink, checking it is well covered and stamp onto the apron. Continue stamping with the corn and artichoke stamps in the same way, re-inking the stamps for each print. If the motifs begin to show signs of lightening, apply more ink to the ink pad. Clean the stamps at regular intervals with stamp cleaner to maintain a clear image.

**❺** Pour the fabric paints into bowls or a palette. Have a jar of water on hand to wash the brush between colors. Apply paint to each motif with a sable brush. To shade or to darken a color, go over the same area twice.

**❻** When dry, iron on the reverse, if necessary, to set the fabric paint.

# Furniture & Accessories

# TABLE LAMP

MATERIALS

✳

Fine sandpaper

✳

Table lamp

✳

"JOIE" stamp

✳

Paintbrush

✳

Acrylic paints:

*Venetian red, yellow*

*ocher, raw umber,*

*white*

✳

Small roller and

paint tray or a plate

✳

Damp cloth

✳

Gold marker pen

*This pretty little table lamp lends itself to a simple but elegant design. Painted first in Venetian red, it was then stamped with curling letters in cream, to match the lampshade. To tie it all together, the same design was stamped along both edges of the lampshade in Venetian red to match the base of the lamp. A touch of gold lining on the base strengthens its contours, draws attention to decorative detail, and adds a sense of style to the completed table lamp.*

**1** Before painting, lightly sand the table lamp using fine sandpaper. Wipe clean with a damp cloth to remove any dust and, when dry, paint with Venetian red acrylic paint. Allow the first coat to dry completely before applying the second coat.

**2** Squeeze 2in. (5cm) of white acrylic paint onto the paint tray, adding a spot each of yellow ocher and raw umber and renewing, as necessary. Mix well until the desired color is reached. For even coverage, transfer the paint to the stamp by rolling the roller across it once or twice.

**3** Hold the lamp securely and stamp with care, applying pressure evenly. Any mistakes should be wiped off immediately with a damp cloth. Re-ink stamp as required and continue to the end of the row. Wait until the first row has dried before beginning the next or you may smudge your work.

4 Using a gold marker pen, draw lines around the base and top of the lamp - the grooves in the lamp will help to guide your hand while you are doing this.

MATERIALS
*
Venetian red acrylic
paint
*
Lampshade
*
Roller and paint tray
or plate
*
Stamp of elaborate
design

# LAMP SHADE

*A quick and stylish solution to finding a lampshade to go with your favorite lamp base is to transform a plain lampshade with an elegant calligraphic stamp. Here the Venetian red stamping complements the print on the lamp base. The same stamp, printed in a different color and arranged in an alternative way, would go equally well with almost any lamp base, provided the colors blend with your base.*

**A lamp to add a touch of class to your room. Stamped with calligraphic letters on a rich Venetian red background, this elegant table lamp and matching shade would sit happily in any setting.**

1 Mix Venetian red acrylic paint as for the table lamp. Place your hand inside the lampshade behind where the top row will be stamped. Stamp against your hand – this gives you a firm base against which to press. Continue around the edge. Repeat the process around the lower edge.

# MIRROR

MATERIALS

✳

**Mirror with wooden frame**

✳

**Black matte oil paint and paintbrush**

✳

**Gold acrylic paint**

✳

**Paint tray or plate**

✳

**Small roller**

✳

**Handmade sun stamp (see Templates)**

✳

**Spare paper**

✳

**Stamp with snowflakes pattern**

✳

**Damp cloth**

✳

**Furniture polish and soft cloth (optional)**

✳

**Varnish and paintbrush**

*T*his large mirror lends itself to a simple but distinctive image and is decorated with a homemade stamp, combined with a ready-made stamp. I have stamped gold on black to create a rich, sumptuous look – but there are many alternatives that would look equally exciting: yellow ocher on a moody blue-green background; or dull blue-gray with a red ocher motif; while two different whites, lime-white on an antique white background would create a cool, delicate style. Experiment with acrylic paint on pieces of cardboard or scraps of wood.

❶ Sand the frame, then paint it with two coats of black matte oil paint. Squeeze 2in. (5cm) of gold acrylic paint onto a paint tray or plate, renewing it as it is needed, so it does not dry out. Roll the roller through the paint several times until it is evenly covered.

**TIP** Acrylic paint dries fairly quickly, so there is less chance of smudging when applying a second stamp. However, it will also dry on brushes and rollers, so always wash your equipment as soon as you have finished. If you are stamping an object that will take some time, check the equipment for signs of drying out. If it does start to dry, wash in warm, soapy water and prepare some more.

❷ Roll the roller once or twice over the handmade sun stamp to give an even covering of paint. Test the stamp first on a spare piece of paper to check you are using the correct amount of paint for a clear image.

**3** Stamp the sun carefully onto the frame. Continue stamping all the way around. In this case, I have stamped only half of the sun onto the mirror – this makes stamping easier, and any variations in size only add to the charm.

**4** Roll gold paint onto the snowflakes stamp and fill in the gaps between the suns. Any mistakes while stamping should be wiped off immediately with a damp cloth.

**5** When all the gold paint is dry, wipe the mirror with a little mineral spirits to remove any fingermarks and then varnish it.

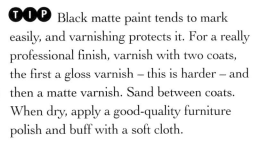

**TIP** Black matte paint tends to mark easily, and varnishing protects it. For a really professional finish, varnish with two coats, the first a gloss varnish – this is harder – and then a matte varnish. Sand between coats. When dry, apply a good-quality furniture polish and buff with a soft cloth.

**Decorative and dramatic in black, this mirror is embellished with resplendent suns and tiny snowflake motifs.**

# PLACEMATS

*When combined with a special paint finish, stamps can offer even more interesting effects – blending with the finish to give a muted subtlety, providing a strong contrast or balancing a colourful background. Fun and yet simple to do, the paint finish on these placemats will intrigue your guests and grace the most elegant dinner table. The gold stamped letters add a touch of sophistication to complete the effect.*

**TIP** The secret of this paint finish is to work quickly, keeping the surface wet until the gold is sprayed over the varnish.

**1** Paint the blue and yellow ocher varnish onto the surface of the placemats, working quickly so they don't have time to dry.

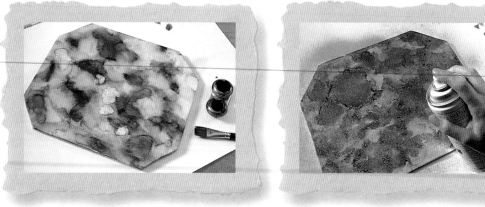

**2** Dip the blending brush into the denatured alcohol and blend in the two colors together evenly.

**3** While the surface is still wet, spray gold paint quickly over the entire surface. If the gold is sprayed on too heavily, it will obscure the colors underneath. Leave to dry.

MATERIALS

✳

**White placemats**

✳

**French enamel varnish in blue and yellow ocher**

✳

**Two cheap bristle brushes reserved for French enamel varnish**

✳

**Brush for blending**

✳

**Denatured alcohol in jar**

✳

**Gold spray**

✳

**Ruler and pencil**

✳

**Acrylic paints:**

*Hooker's green, cobalt blue, white, gold*

✳

**Artist's bristle brush**

✳

**Gold marker pen**

✳

**Stamp with elaborate design**

✳

**Small paint roller and paint tray or plate**

**4** Measure a 1½in. (3.8cm) border around the edge of the mat. Mix together 2 in. (5cm) of Hooker's green and cobalt blue with ½in. (1cm) of white and paint in a border. Using a ruler and a gold marker pen, draw a single gold line along the inner edge.

**TIP** If white mats are difficult to find, make your own with hardboard. Make a template using an old tablemat and cut them out with a craft knife on a cutting mat. Sand the surface and paint with two coats of flat white oil paint. When finished, glue green felt to the underside to protect your table.

Alternatively, first sand the surface of colored or old tablemats and paint with two coats of flat white oil paint.

**5** Squeeze out 2in. (5cm) of gold paint onto a plate. Cover the stamp with gold, using the roller. Stamp onto the green border. For a perfect fit, use cutout stamps arranged on top of the border first, marking their places with a soft pencil.

**These stylish placemats, a sea of glorious colors and stamped in gold, will enhance any table for special occasions.**

# TRAY

**MATERIALS**

✳

**Tray, painted white**

✳

**Artist's oil paints:**
*phthalo blue, golden yellow, burnt umber, burnt sienna, permanent rose, raw umber*

✳

**Paint tray or large white plate**

✳

**Paintbrushes**

✳

**Mineral spirits**

✳

**White matte decorator's paint**

✳

**Orchid botanical stamp (or other flower)**

✳

**Several sheets of strong, thin paper such as typing paper**

✳

**Black fabric ink pad**

✳

**Art brush pens:**
*wine red, light ocher, magenta, mist purple, black and teal green*

✳

**Semi-matte and gloss varnish**

✳

**Craft knife and cutting mat**

✳

**Repositioning and permanent glue**

✳

**French polish, soft cloth, and fine sandpaper (optional)**

✳

**Furniture polish**

*Découpage has enjoyed a revival in the last few years – and deservedly so. It is fun to do, does not require any specialist techniques or artistic abilities, and is relatively inexpensive. Originating in the seventeenth century, découpage sought to imitate the hand-painted Japanese and Chinese lacquerwork that was then being imported into Europe. This red and black lacquer furniture proved to be so popular that demand far outstripped supply, so craftsmen were employed to imitate the technique. Hand painting soon gave way to the use of paper cutouts and was executed on more modest pieces of furniture. The word découpage comes from the French word* découper *– to cut out.*

Stamps add a new dimension to découpage. You can stamp your own prints, color them, and cut them out rather than searching in magazines for images. Traditionally, découpage was applied only to red or black backgrounds, but there is no reason why you cannot use any colored background or, as in the case of this tray, a simple paint finish.

**1** Put 1½in. (3.8cm) of phthalo blue and golden yellow on a paint tray or plate and add ½in. (1.3cm) of burnt umber. With a paintbrush, blend together with a little mineral spirits. Add the mixture to white decorator's paint and mix well. Paint the base of the tray and leave to dry. Apply a second coat and leave to dry.

Add white to the mix until it is much paler and, with a dry brush, cover the base coat, allowing the color to show through. The brush should not be too heavily coated with paint, as the aim is to create a broken finish.

**2** Mix 2in. (5cm) of burnt sienna and permanent rose, adding ¼in. (6mm) of white. Paint the edge and outer sides of the tray.

**3** Stamp eight motifs of Orchid onto the paper using a black fabric ink pad.

**4** Color in the motifs using the various art brush pens.

**TIP** Varnish when the glue is dry. Traditional découpage was varnished with as many as thirty coats of varnish, but you can use French polish to achieve a pleasing effect with six to ten layers. Pour equal amounts of French polish and denatured alcohol into a container. Wipe on quickly with a soft, lint-free cloth. Leave for one hour. Apply subsequent coats, sanding lightly in between. Finish with two coats of matte varnish and, when dry, polish with a good-quality furniture polish.

**5** Varnish each motif with one coat of semi-matte varnish. Leave to dry.

**6** Using a craft knife on a cutting mat, carefully cut out each image.

PAINTBOX

To obtain exactly the color I wanted, I used 8oz. (250ml) of white matte oil-based decorator's paint and colored it with artist's oil colors; otherwise, use a ready-colored paint.

**7** Arrange the motifs on the tray using repositioning glue. When you are pleased with the effect, glue them firmly into place. When the glue is dry, varnish.

**Decorate a tray for all occasions with pretty découpage magnolias.**

# CLOCK

**MATERIALS**
∗
**Wooden clock**
∗
**Decorator's tape**
∗
**Acrylic paints:** *yellow ocher, white*
∗
**Fine sandpaper**
∗
**Paint trays or plates**
∗
**Two small paintbrushes**
∗
**Large round bristle brush**
∗
**Black fabric paint pad and ink**
∗
**Victorian border and fruit stamps (grapes are used here)**
∗
**Clear varnish**

*D*ecorated clocks are much in demand nowadays. There is every imaginable style to choose from – zany fluorescent, stark geometric, pretty floral, or the more traditional which I have chosen to do here. Stamping can accommodate almost any style; when combined with a paint technique, the range is boundless. The delicate two-tone effect on this clock is easily obtained by stippling a darker-tinted glaze over the background color, so that it resembles the lustrous satin-like sheen of satinwood. Stamping in black complements the design of the clock face.

**1** Protect the clock face with decorator's tape. On a paint tray or plate, mix 3 in. (7.5cm) of yellow ocher acrylic paint from a tube with a tiny amount of white and paint the clock. Leave to dry and sand lightly. Apply a second coat and sand again.

**2** Pour the glaze onto a paint tray or large plate. With the bristle brush, stipple the glaze onto the clock by rotating the brush each time to create an uneven effect. Leave to dry.

**3** Using the fabric ink pad and the Victorian border stamp, apply the design carefully around the edge of the clock.

## GLAZE RECIPE

✱

**Artist's oil paints:**

*yellow ocher, raw umber,*

*Venetian red*

✱

**old jar**

✱

**1 tbsp. mineral spirits**

✱

**2 tbsp. transparent**

**oil glaze**

Squeeze ½ in. (1.25cm) of raw umber paint into an old jar, add ¼ in. (6mm) of yellow ocher and a dot of Venetian red. Add the mineral spirits and, with an old brush, mix until completely smooth. Add the transparent oil glaze and mix.

**Stamp a clock to be proud of, with this traditional Victorian border motif.**

❹ With the grapes (or other fruit) stamp and the same inked pad, stamp a row of grapes under the clock face.

When dry, apply a coat of varnish. (Transparent oil glaze is a soft glaze so it needs to be protected.)

# EGG CUPBOARD

*This charming little holder is for keeping eggs and seems to suggest a rustic finish in keeping with its country style. It is the perfect size, too, for trying your hand at a new technique before moving on to a larger piece of furniture. If an egg cupboard proves difficult to find, the same process could be applied to any small wall or corner cupboard.*

## PAINTBOX

Vinyl latex is used for the base coat and the inside of the cupboard. Pickling paste is available from paint stores; it is water-based and simple to use. For the rooster and the top rim, I have used acrylic paint.

**1** Lightly sand the surface of the cupboard before painting. Paint the inside and outside of the cupboard with two coats of the dark blue vinyl latex, leaving it to dry between coats. Paint the rim with white acrylic paint.

**2** When dry, apply an even coat of pickling paste on the outside. Leave the inside dark blue and leave to dry.

**3** With the medium-grade steel wool, gently rub off the pickling paste from the surface to reveal the color and grain of the wood underneath. Maintain an even pressure, so the finished effect is not too regular or patchy.

**4** Squeeze out 2in. (5cm) each of burnt sienna and permanent rose acrylic paint, add a dash of white on a plate, and mix well with a palette knife. Paint the rim around the top of the cupboard.

**5** Apply red paint to the rooster stamp with a small roller. Check that it is evenly covered. Before stamping onto the cupboard, try it out on a similar surface first.

**6** Reapply the paint and stamp two roosters on both sides of the cupboard. Stamp the top of the egg cupboar

**A stamped rooster over a decorative paint finish transforms this pretty cupboard into something special.**

*You can transform your home with stamping. Use it for decorative
chinaware, which you can display on a hutch like this one, or for useful
items around the house, such as utensil boxes and an egg cupboard.*

*Add individual style to a living room with elegant stamped furniture. An old chair can be completely revamped by stamping; and mirrors, lamps, and clocks can be decorated to coordinate with your decor. As a finishing touch, stamp a wastepaper basket.*

# CHAIR

*H*ere is a sumptuous way of rescuing an old chair destined for the scrap heap, or perhaps one that was just uninteresting to start with. There is no need to spend hours doing it up first. Applying gold découpage motifs rather than stamping them straight onto the chair produces a facsimile of burnished gesso. Gesso originated in Italy where it was used as a ground on which to apply gold leaf where the surface was rough, creating a smooth slightly raised area which insured a gleaming gold decoration.

## PAINTBOX

Matte black oil paint is used to paint the chair, and you should always stir it well before use. The quality of the base coat here is important so, before applying the découpage stamps, spend time on obtaining a really fine paint surface. Imperfections on the chair itself lend appeal, but a poorly painted finish will spoil the effect. For the découpage stamps, a mixture of white glue and gold metallic powder is used. If you can't find this, antique gold acrylic will do the job. The final effect will be less lustrous but pretty nonetheless. For the glue and gold powder mixture, mix 2 tablespoons of glue to 1 tablespoon of water in an old jar and stir thoroughly. Add 1 teaspoon of gold metallic powder carefully. It is very fine and will end up in everything if it is spilled. Mix thoroughly with a spoon and pour onto a paint tray or a plate.

**1** Sand the chair before painting. Use a coarse grade if it is in a poor state, followed by a medium grade, and finishing with a fine grade. Clean with a cloth and mineral spirits before painting.

**2** To achieve a really lustrous finish, apply four coats of black matte oil paint. Leave to dry between each coat and sand with fine-grade sandpaper. You can use a brush or a small roller, but remember to clean them with mineral spirits after use.

**3** Apply one coat of gloss varnish, leave to dry, and sand lightly before applying two coats of matte varnish, sanding between each coat. Leave to dry.

MATERIALS
*
Chair
*
Sandpaper – coarse, medium, and fine grade
*
Mineral spirits and cloth
*
Black matte oil paint
*
Paintbrushes: 2 1-in. (2.5-cm) decorator's brushes
*
Small roller and paint tray or plate
*
Gloss and matte varnish
*
White craft glue
*
Gold metallic powder
*
Ivy leaf stamp
*
Good-quality white paper
*
Fabric ink - any color
*
Cutting board and craft knife
*
Repositioning glue
*
Craft glue
*
Gold felt-tip pen

Découpage leaves stamped in gold give a dramatic look to a simple black chair.

**4** Using a small roller, apply the glue and metallic powder mixture or gold paint (see Paintbox) to the ivy leaf stamp. Stamp onto white paper. Re-ink and stamp eight motifs onto white paper – or however many you need for your particular chair. Leave to dry completely. Stamp *one* motif in fabric ink.

**5** When they are completely dry, cut out the ivy leaf motifs on a cutting mat, using a craft knife. When cutting out any motifs, always cut carefully and away from your body to avoid an accident. Cut out the plain inked motif, turn it over, and paint the *back* with the glue mixture or gold paint using a small paintbrush.

**6** Use repositioning glue while you arrange the motifs on the chair until you are pleased with the effect. The separate painted motif is to use on the back rest to create a symmetrical design. The motifs can also be cut to fit symmetrically, if preferred. On the backrest of this chair, a single leaf has been cut from a spare motif and placed in the center to complete the design.

**7** Using an all-purpose craft glue, stick the motifs firmly into place. Apply four coats of matte varnish and leave to dry.

**8** Apply several coats of good-quality furniture polish and buff to a rich shine.

**9** Using a gold felt-tip pen, apply gold lines on the backrest above the design and on any carved features on the supports.

# COFFEE TABLE

*A coffee table is an ideal piece of furniture if you want to try stamping on a large scale. Here, a modest coffee table is transformed with stunning "primitive" stamps, printed in black over an oil-glaze paint finish. The same paint finish and stamps could be used with other colors to create a completely different effect. The permutations are practically endless – have fun and experiment.*

## PAINTBOX

The base coat of the table was painted with eggshell oil paint. Eggshell gives a good base on which to apply a glaze and makes the glaze more workable. Glazes can dry quickly in a warm atmosphere, so it is important to work fairly quickly and all at once, or there will be "tide" marks. For the same reason, do not go over the same area twice, or the glaze will build up and look uneven.

## GLAZE RECIPE

Equal parts of: transparent oil glaze and mineral spirits
Artist's oil paints: raw umber, yellow ocher
Mineral spirits
Jam jar or paint kettle

The amounts you need will vary according to the size of your table, but 1 pint (½ litre) of the fully mixed glaze should be enough for most coffee tables.

Pour equal amounts of transparent oil glaze and mineral spirits into a container and stir until well mixed, using an old brush. Squeeze equal amounts of raw umber and yellow ocher into a jar or paint bucket, blend thoroughly with a little more mineral spirits, just enough to mix it well. Add 2 tablespoons of the glaze mixture and, when well mixed, pour in the rest. To check the color, try out the tinted glaze on white painted board.

**1** Paint the table with two coats of white eggshell oil paint. Leave to dry and lightly sand between coats.

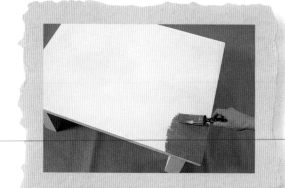

**2** Apply one coat of the tinted glaze with a brush. Work quickly. Do one area of the table at a time. Immediately, with the fitch brush, go over the glazed surface with stabbing movements, or a rough stippling. Repeat on the next area of the table until the entire table has been stippled. Leave for 24 hours until completely dry.

MATERIALS

✳

**Coffee table**

✳

**½ gallon (2.5 litre) can eggshell white oil paint**

✳

**Sandpaper – fine grade**

✳

**Brushes: 2 decorator's brushes, 1in. (2.5cm) and 2in. (5cm); I fitch brush**

✳

**2 Primitive-style stamps and 1 home-made eraser stamp**

✳

**Black acrylic paints**

✳

**Small roller and paint tray or plate**

✳

**Matte and gloss varnish**

✳

**Furniture polish**

**3** Apply black acrylic paint to the primitive stamp with the small roller. Try it out on a piece of scrap paper first to insure the paint is evenly distributed.

**4** Stamp onto the table. With large stamps, care must be taken to insure they print evenly, so press firmly first in the middle of the stamp and then the sides without rocking the stamp.

**5** Apply black paint to the second stamp and print it next to the first. Practice stamping the two stamps side by side on a piece of paper.

**7** Apply one coat of gloss varnish to the whole table. When it is completely dry, sand with a fine-grade sandpaper and give the table a second coat with matte varnish. When dry, polish with furniture polish.

**Ethnic stamps, combined with a stippled paint finish, create a stylish coffee table.**

**6** Apply the black paint to the small hand-made stamp and print along the side of the table. Leave to dry. Apply the same stamp to the legs of the table.

# STOOL

*A high stool, an invaluable perch in any kitchen, can be painted to match the decor or to provide a contrast to existing colors. Both decorative and useful, it adds a little something to the kitchen as well as being ideal to stamp on. A simple star, which will successfully integrate with almost any other design, is stamped on the top.*

## PAINTBOX
The stool is painted first in "old white" flat oil paint. Around the edge of the top, a dark blue circle has been painted, a mixture of 2in. (5cm) each of phthalo blue and burnt umber artist's oil paint and 2 tablespoons of "old white." This was also used for the carved areas on the legs. Over this was stippled a dark maroon/burgundy red in flat oil paint.

**1** Apply two coats of "old white" flat oil paint to the stool with a decorator's brush. This creamy white paint gives an antique look. Leave to dry and sand between coats with a fine-grade sandpaper.

**3** Stamp seven stars onto white paper using the fabric ink. Cut them out on a cutting mat using a craft knife. Arrange and, with repositioning glue, anchor them into place around the top of the stool.

**2** Using the artist's bristle brush, paint a circle of the blue paint mixture around the outer edge of the stool. Don't worry too much about making it perfect – the final effect will conceal any wobbly edges.

**4** Apply the maroon or burgundy paint to the entire stool with the fitch brush, stippling over the stars on the top of the stool. Leave to dry, then remove the paper stars to expose white stars beneath.

## MATERIALS
*
**Stool**
*
**"Old white" flat oil paint**
*
**Brushes: 2 1-in. (2.5cm) decorator's brushes; 2 artist's bristle brushes, size 8; artist's brush, size 2; fitch brush**
*
**Fine-grade sandpaper**
*
**Artist's oil paint:**
*phthalo blue, burnt umber*
*
**Star stamp**
*
**Fabric ink – any color**
*
**Cutting mat and knife**
*
**Repositioning glue**
*
**Mineral spirits**
*
**Dark maroon or burgundy red flat oil paint**
*
**Turquoise acrylic paint**
*
**Small roller and paint tray or plate**

**5** Apply turquoise acrylic paint to the star stamp with a small roller. Stamp first onto a scrap of paper to check the coverage is even.

**6** Line up the star stamp with the exposed star on top of the stool and stamp firmly. Wipe off any mistakes immediately with a damp cloth as acrylic paint dries quickly.

**7** Thin the burgundy or maroon paint slightly with mineral spirits. Then using a small artist's sable or synthetic brush, paint the white areas inside the stars.

**The stool to catch the eye, stippled in maroon with a cluster of turquoise stars.**

# WORKBOX

*This modest little workbox provides an ideal object to try your hand at simulating lacquerwork. The art of lacquering was first developed in China. By the fifteenth century, Japanese lacquering had transcended that of the Chinese, and most of the lacquerwork imported to Europe originated in Japan.*

**MATERIALS**

✳

**Wooden workbox**

✳

**Acrylic paints:** *burnt sienna, permanent rose, yellow ocher, gold*

✳

**Large plates**

✳

**Paintbrush**

✳

**600 wet and dry sandpaper**

✳

**French polish**

✳

**Denatured alcohol**

✳

**Soft cotton cloth**

✳

**Very fine steel wool**

✳

**Clear gloss varnish (optional)**

✳

**Small roller and paint tray**

✳

**Leaf stamp (an oak leaf is used here)**

✳

**Wet cloth**

✳

**Gold marker pen**

✳

**Fine sandpaper**

A lacquer finish has a flawless, gleaming surface. Traditionally, this was created by applying up to forty layers of prepared resin from the lac tree, *Rhus vernicifera*, each layer being polished and perfected before the next was applied. "Japanning" was the name later given to the imitation lacquer developed by English craftsmen responding to the huge demand in Europe. Over the centuries, various techniques were developed in Europe aimed at reproducing oriental lacquerwork, each with its own distinctive charm – so it would be quite in keeping to try your hand at this simple piece, requiring just a little time and patience.

**1** Put equal amounts of burnt sienna and permanent rose acrylic paints on a plate, mix with a paintbrush and add a small amount of yellow ocher. For a really rich color, paint the workbox with four or five coats. Leave to dry between each coat and sand with wet and dry paper before applying the next.

**2** Dilute the French polish with the same amount of denatured alcohol on a plate. Using a piece of soft cotton – it must be smooth and lint free – apply the French polish quickly. Leave to dry and then rub the surface with very fine steel wool. Repeat this process between six and ten times.

You can finish with a coat of clear gloss varnish, again rubbing down with the wet and dry paper.

**3** Put some gold acrylic paint on a paint tray or large plate. Use the roller to cover the leaf stamp and stamp carefully onto the workbox. Such a shiny surface can be slippery, so it needs a steady hand. Keep a wet cloth on hand to wipe off any mistakes.

**4** With a gold marker pen, highlight the edges of the workbox using the carved indentations on the box as a guide to insure a firm, even line.

**The finished workbox, gleaming red and extravagantly pretty, stamped with simple gold oak leaves. Deceptively simple to do, this decorative treatment turns an otherwise modest box into something precious and important.**

# FIRESCREEN

*F*irescreens – which give an empty fireplace a stylish look during the summer months – are enjoying something of a revival. They are also wonderful to decorate and you can even decorate one to resemble an old heirloom. Combined with a paint finish, the effect can be stunning.

## PAINTBOX

I have used flat oil paints to paint the base colors on the firescreen. Flat oil paints are not always easy to find, and you can substitute latex paint. The colors you will need if you use latex paint are: a reddish-brown for the first coat and a mid-green for the second. The gold fleur-de-lys are painted with gold acrylic. Alternatively, use 1 teaspoon of gold metallic powder stirred, with care, into 1 tablespoon of white glue and paint it on in the same way. The result is quite beautiful.

### MATERIALS FOR MAKING THE FIRESCREEN

✳

**Sheet of brown paper, twice the size of the firescreen**

✳

**Sheet of MDF 2 x 2ft (60 x 60cm)**

✳

**Medium and fine-grade sandpaper**

✳

**Wood glue**

✳

**Wood clamps**

✳

**Workbench or old table**

✳

**Jigsaw**

## TO MAKE THE FIRESCREEN

**1** Fold the sheet of brown paper in half and draw on the shape of the firescreen (see templates). Cut out the brown paper shape. Open the pattern and place on the sheet of composition board. Secure the paper with thumbtacks and draw carefully around it.

**2** Using clamps, attach the firescreen firmly to a workbench or table, insuring that the edge of the board is free of it.

**3** Using the jigsaw, carefully cut out the edges of the firescreen, moving and re-clamping it, as necessary. Sand the entire screen, first with medium-grade sandpaper, then with fine-grade sandpaper.

**4** Copy the pattern for the back supports (see templates) and transfer to the board, cutting it out the same way as the firescreen.

**5** Place the firescreen face down on a firm, even surface. Glue both back supports onto the back of the screen (see templates) with wood glue. Leave to dry, according to the manufacturer's instructions.

### MATERIALS

✳

**Firescreen**

✳

**Small bristle decorator's brushes**

✳

**1 small can of** *Etruscan red* **paint in flat oil**

✳

**Wax candle**

✳

**1 small can of** *green smoke* **paint in flat oil**

✳

**Several sheets of white paper**

✳

**Scissors**

✳

**Stamps:** *fleur-de-lys and small flower*

✳

**Acrylic paints:** *Antique gold, maroon, Venetian red*

✳

**Small roller and paint tray or plate**

✳

**Fine steel wool**

✳

**Sable paint brush, size 4**

✳

**Good-quality wax furniture polish**

Gold fleur-de-lys decorate this attractive firescreen with a distressed finish.

**1** Paint both sides and edges of the firescreen in Etruscan red. Leave to dry.

Rub over the entire screen unevenly with a wax candle and leave for one hour.

**2** Paint the entire screen in green smoke. Leave to dry.

**3** Stamp some fleur-de-lys in maroon paint onto paper. Cut out and arrange on the screen. Remove them, making a mark under each as a guide to stamping.

**4** Using the small roller, apply maroon acrylic paint to the fleur-de-lys stamp. Stamp the front of the screen on the marks, re-applying paint for each motif.

**5** With very fine steel wool, randomly rub away paint to reveal the layers underneath. Be careful when rubbing over the motifs. Ideally, you want to reveal some of the color beneath, not rub away your work.

**6** With a wash of gold acrylic and a sable brush, paint over the fleur-de-lys. If you opt for the gold powder and glue, paint over the motifs unevenly, insuring the color underneath shows in patches. Omit stage 7.

**7** Using a thicker consistency of gold acrylic, paint fine lines on some of the edges of the motif to create a shadow effect.

**8** Apply maroon paint to small flower stamp and print between the fleur-de-lys.

**9** Paint the edges of the firescreen with gold acrylic paint. When all the paint is dry, polish with furniture polish.

# CUP AND SAUCER

MATERIALS
✳
**Cup and saucer**
✳
**Ceramic paints:**
*old rose, yellow ochre*
*and blue*
✳
**2 artist's paint**
**brushes, size 4**
✳
**Artist's paint brush,**
**size 2**
✳
**Folk Basket stamp**

*T*he versatility of stamping is shown particularly well by ceramic ware. This decorative cup and saucer would make a fine display in a kitchen or corner cupboard. Once you have mastered the technique, you could stamp an entire tea set! It must be emphasized, however, that the paints used here are purely decorative. Do not use stamped china for eating and drinking.

## CREATIVE STAMPING

The shape of the cup and saucer here, with its natural ridges, lends itself to stripes of alternating colors. If you are unable to find a similar shape, the same effect can be achieved by using a cup with straight sides and masking tape. First you will need to plan where to put the masking tape. Turn the cup upside-down on a clean sheet of paper and draw around the rim, cut out the circle, and fold it in half, then in half again, to give you eight sections. Tape it to the top of the cup and mark the sections with a soft pencil. Use the handle as a starting point so that one stripe has the handle in the middle – it will be awkward to paint two different colors with the handle in the middle of them. Stick four pieces of masking tape firmly to the sides of the cup with four alternating strips between them. An alternative to masking tape is masking paper which can be cut to size.

**1** Mask four alternating sections with the masking tape. Paint the four unmasked sections with yellow ocher, using a size 4 paintbrush and taking care not to smudge the paint as you go along. Leave to dry. It should be dry enough to continue in four hours and will be completely dry in 24 hours.

**A decorative gem with lovely colors and a simple stamp.**

**2** While the cup is drying, you can begin the saucer. Using a size 4 paintbrush, paint the center in old rose. Leave to dry, then carefully paint yellow ocher around the edge.

**3** Remove the masking tape on the cup and paint the four remaining sections with old rose. Leave to dry.

**4** Turn the cup upside down and paint the lower section blue (size 2 brush). Leave to dry for four hours. Paint the edge of the saucer blue. Turn the cup up and paint the rim in blue (size 2 brush). Leave to dry.

**5** Apply blue ceramic paint to the stamp with a bristle brush. Print first on a piece of paper to remove excess paint, then placing the cup upside down on a firm surface, stamp onto the cup. Continue around the cup, working on alternating sections to avoid smudging.

PAINTBOX

The development of cold ceramic paints has opened up new possibilities, enabling those of us without access to a kiln to try our hand at a new craft. Water-based ceramic paints, as used here, are specially formulated to use on glazed ceramics. After 24 hours' drying time, their durability is improved by hardening them in a kitchen oven. Always check the manufacturer's instructions for temperature and time, as some brands of cold ceramic paints do not require any heating.

# LARGE PLATE

MATERIALS

❋

**Large white plate**

❋

**Tracing paper**

❋

**Soft pencil**

❋

**White paper**

❋

**Bath sponge**

❋

**Scissors**

❋

**Sponge head of**

**small roller**

❋

**Ceramic paints:** *wine*

*and yellow ocher*

❋

**Plates for paint**

*A bath sponge and a little paint is all you need to transform a plain white plate into an eye-catching creation. You can transform your kitchen with a display of cheap white plates stamped either in the same colors and shapes or with different colors. Use vibrant colors or soft pastels, dramatic dark blue and gold – have some fun and experiment with different designs and colors.*

PAINTBOX

Water-based ceramic paints are specially formulated for use on glazed ceramics. Always read the manufacturer's instructions to check whether or not they need to be hardened in a kitchen oven. It is important to remember that these paints are used for decorative purposes *only* and should not come in contact with food. They can be washed gently, but won't stand up to dishwashers or scrubbing.

❶ Trace the three shapes from the templates and transfer them onto a piece of paper. Cut them out and place them on top of the sponge. Dampen slightly to stay in place. With a pair of scissors, cut out your sponge stamp. The sponge head of a small roller removed from its handle will serve as a fourth stamp.

❷ Pour wine and yellow ocher ceramic paint onto two separate plates. Spread the paint evenly with a small roller.

❸ Dip the round roller head into the wine ceramic paint. Check it is evenly covered. Practice stamping on a spare plate first.

❹ Press onto the edge of the center of the plate. Re-dip and stamp evenly around the plate. Mistakes can be wiped off while wet.

**5** Dip the triangular sponge stamp into the wine ceramic paint. Check it is evenly covered and stamp around the edge of the plate. Don't worry about small overlaps or gaps – the overall look is one of informality.

**6** Dip the small round sponge into the wine-colored ceramic paint. You should check that it is evenly covered and stamp it around the plate between the triangles.

**A plain white plate transformed with handmade stamps made from an ordinary household sponge.**

**7** Dip the oblong stamp into the yellow ocher ceramic paint. Check it is evenly covered and stamp between the large circles joining them all up.

**8** Dip the unused end of the small round sponge into the yellow ocher ceramic paint. Check that it is evenly colored and stamp beneath the small wine-colored dots.

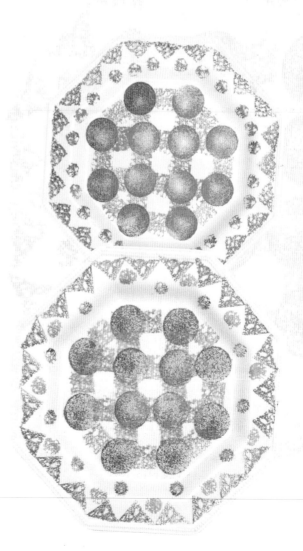

# LARGE PITCHER

*Transform an ordinary pitcher with two simple homemade sponge stamps – a quick and effortless technique that is particularly attractive. You will want to stamp more – a set of pitchers, perhaps, in different colors or mugs to match. Homemade sponge stamps are ideal for stamping onto ceramics as they mold themselves easily around curved hard surfaces.*

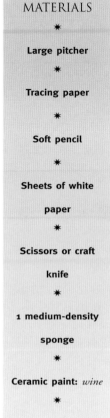

## MATERIALS

*

**Large pitcher**

*

**Tracing paper**

*

**Soft pencil**

*

**Sheets of white paper**

*

**Scissors or craft knife**

*

**1 medium-density sponge**

*

**Ceramic paint:** *wine*

*

**Large white plate**

## PAINTBOX

The paints used for the pitcher are water-based ceramic paints, especially formulated for use on glazed ceramics. Always check the manufacturer's instructions before use, as some, but not all, need to be hardened in a kitchen oven. Remember, though, that these paints are purely for decorative purposes and should not come in contact with food.

**1** Trace the two heart shapes from the templates and transfer them onto the white paper. Cut them out and place them on top of the sponge. Dampen the paper hearts slightly to make them stick to the sponge and stay in place. With a sharp pair of scissors, cut out your sponge stamps.

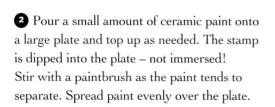

**2** Pour a small amount of ceramic paint onto a large plate and top up as needed. The stamp is dipped into the plate – not immersed! Stir with a paintbrush as the paint tends to separate. Spread paint evenly over the plate.

**3** Dip the large sponge heart into the paint, checking that it is evenly covered. Try it out first on a piece of spare paper.

**4** Stamp the base of the pitcher, starting at one side of the handle and continue stamping around the base until you reach the other side. Don't worry if the motifs overlap – the charm of this design is its informality. When you have finished the bottom row, begin the next row up, starting again at the handle. Re-dip the sponge after every second print, taking care, as you go, not to smudge your work.

**5** Dip the small sponge heart into the paint. Check that it is evenly covered, trying it out first on a piece of spare paper, as before.

**6** Starting at the lip of the pitcher, print a row all around the top section. You should continue printing in rows until the pitcher is completed.

**Deceptively easy, these simple hearts are stamped with a sponge onto a pitcher and look strikingly effective.**

# SMALL KITCHEN BASKET

*O*nce the domain of servants, kitchens are now often the focal point of our homes, the cozy center for family and friends to get together in a warm, friendly atmosphere. Whether you want a simple modern kitchen, one with a "period feel," or something more sophisticated, you will inevitably have an array of cooking utensils, pottery, and china on display – all of which can be decorated with attractive and eye-catching stamps.

## PAINTBOX

Acrylic paints are ideal for small items as they dry so quickly as well as having a vast color range. They are water soluble, but the finish is tough and will stand up to repeated use. Always clean stamps with stamp cleaner after use. Brushes, too, will be ruined if allowed to dry with paint on – so you should wash them immediately after use.

**MATERIALS**

✳

**Small flat basket**

✳

**Acrylic paints:**

*golden ocher, cadmium yellow, phthalo blue, burnt umber, and titanium white*

✳

**Sandpaper**

✳

**Small roller and paint tray or plate**

✳

**Artist's bristle brush size 6**

✳

**Scherenschnitte (an urn with flowers in a folk art design) and Heart Stencil stamps**

✳

**Sheet of white paper**

✳

**Scissors**

✳

**Repositioning glue**

✳

**Water and mineral spirits for cleaning**

✳

**Fabric pen:** *burgundy*

**① ** Sand the basket. Mix on a paint tray or plate 8in. (20cm) of phthalo blue with 4in. (10cm) of both burnt umber and white. Paint the basket inside and out. Mix 2in. (5cm) of both golden ocher and cadmium yellow, blending them together thoroughly with a drop of water, using a palette knife.

**ⓣⓘⓟ** Always lightly sand any surface to be painted and between coats of paint. A simple way of planning where to stamp the motifs is to first stamp several "Scherenschnitte" on a piece of paper, cut them out, and with a dab of glue arrange them on the basket until you are pleased with the effect. Clean the glue off with mineral spirits before stamping.

**② ** When it is dry, paint the outside slats of the basket yellow, leaving the spaces in between, and the inside the original blue. Paint the inside divider yellow. Leave to dry.

**3** Mix the paint for the stamp using 2in. (5cm) of phthalo blue and 1in. (2.5cm) of burnt umber and white, mixing thoroughly with a palette knife. Using the small roller, apply to the Scherenschnitte stamp, and stamp firmly onto the basket. Reapply the paint and continue to stamp on all four sides.

**4** Apply the blue mixture to the Heart Stencil stamp, and stamp along the top slat on all four sides, reapplying the paint each time. Stamp two motifs on the top of the handle/divider.

**5** Using the burgundy pen, add a touch of red to some of the flowers on the Scherenschnitte motif.

**Hearts and flowers add sparkle to this gaily painted basket.**

# UTENSIL BOX

MATERIALS

\*

**Utensil box painted**

**blue**

\*

**Acrylic paints:**

*golden yellow,*

*cadmium yellow,*

*phthalo blue, burnt*

*umber, and titanium*

*white*

\*

**Scherenschnitte**

**stamp**

\*

**Artist's bristle brush**

**size 6**

\*

**Small roller and**

**paint tray or plate**

\*

**Fabric pen:** *burgundy*

*This pretty little blue and yellow box could be put to many uses in the kitchen for holding candles or general utensils. It has been painted and decorated to match the basket. Paint it yellow, leaving just the edges blue, and use the Scherenschnitte stamp.*

**1** Prepare the box in the same way as the basket, sanding and painting the background color in yellow acrylic paint.

**2** Mix the blue paint as for the basket and apply to the Scherenschnitte stamp.

**3** Stamp firmly on the upper and lower front. With the burgundy pen, add red to the flowers as on the basket.

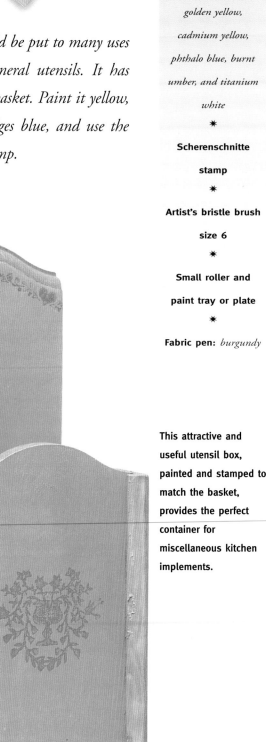

This attractive and useful utensil box, painted and stamped to match the basket, provides the perfect container for miscellaneous kitchen implements.

# WASTEPAPER BASKET

*T*here is every reason to display your wastepaper basket proudly if it is painted and stamped – either to match your furnishings, as an attractive gift for a friend, or just for fun.

## MATERIALS

❋

**2 small rollers and paint trays or plates**

❋

**Black matte oil paint**

❋

**Wastepaper basket**

❋

**Animal stamp (a zebra is used here)**

❋

**White acrylic paint**

❋

**Damp cloth**

❋

**Clear gloss varnish**

**1** With a small roller, give the wastepaper basket two coats of black paint and leave to dry. Use a clean roller to apply white paint onto the stamp. Go over it several times so it is evenly covered.

**2** Holding the wastepaper basket steady, stamp onto it carefully. If your wastebasket is round like this one, you will need to roll the stamp gently from right to left – if you are left-handed from left to right. Keep a damp cloth on hand to wipe off any mistakes.

**3** Give the wastebasket two coats of clear gloss varnish to protect it, allowing the first coat to dry completely before applying the second. A high gloss finish suits the stark black and white.

**A stylish wastebasket in black, stamped with magnificent zebras.**

# For Children

# CHILD'S T-SHIRT

MATERIALS

✳

**White cotton T-shirt**

✳

**Stamps:**

*Pegasus and stars*

✳

**Fabric felt-tip pens:**

*red, yellow, blue,*

*green, purple*

*Stamping for children is great fun – they can choose their own stamp and colors, and even help in the stamping. The felt-tip pens used here are easy for small hands to apply and, being non-toxic, are also safe. There is always a stamp to fit children's ever-changing fads and fantasies – from spooky ghosts and creepy-crawlies to cuddly teddies and dancing pigs. This simple little white T-shirt is stamped with Pegasus, the flying horse.*

PAINTBOX

Fabric felt-tip pens are ideal for printing on white cotton and very simple to use. They are ideal for children – they dry almost immediately, do not fade, the ink is non-toxic, and it is completely washable without any heat setting necessary. For printing on dark colors, fabric paints are more suitable and should be applied to the stamp with a small roller. Always check the manufacturer's instructions to find out whether or not a heat setting is required.

**1** Wash and iron the T-shirt to remove the sizing and place it on a firm, even surface. No planning stage is necessary for this T-shirt, as the stamps are printed at random.

**2** Apply yellow fabric felt tip to the Pegasus stamp. Practice on a scrap of similar fabric.

**3** Place the T-shirt on a firm, even surface. Stamp onto the T-shirt, pressing firmly.

**4** Continue stamping with the green, blue, and red felt tips in the same way, re-inking the stamps for each print. Stamp all the motifs of one color before beginning the next color, spacing them evenly over the T-shirt.

**5** Apply purple fabric felt tip to the stars stamp, insuring that the stamp is well covered with the ink. Before attempting to print on the T-shirt, practice stamping on a scrap of similar fabric.

**The flying horse Pegasus, stamped in several colors, makes a charming, jolly T-shirt for a child.**

**6** Place the T-shirt on a firm, even surface. Stamp the stars onto the T-shirt, placing them between the Pegasus motifs. Re-ink the stamp for each print.

# CHILD'S GYM SHOES

*A*ny child would love these shoes stamped with tiny ladybugs. They could be matched up with the T-shirt or a sun hat or, just for fun, they could all be stamped with different animals, birds, or insects. If you are feeling extravagant, why not stamp a pair of gym shoes to go with different outfits? You could stamp flowers to match a summer dress or tiny shells for a day at the beach.

### PAINTBOX

Fabric inks and fabric felt tips are perfect for stamping on white canvas as they do not need any heat to set the colors. On these shoes, the fabric felt tip is used to color directly onto the canvas.

**1** Apply black ink to the ink pad, massaging in well until fully covered.

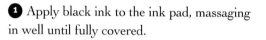

**2** Apply the ink to the ladybug stamp. Check that the ink is spread evenly over the stamp, testing first on a piece of paper. Re-ink for each motif.

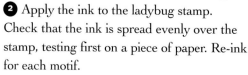

**3** Hold the shoe steady with one hand. Hold the inked stamp with the other hand and print the ladybug onto the canvas, pressing evenly and firmly.

**4** Leave the shoes for about five minutes to make sure they are dry. With a red fabric felt-tip pen, color in the ladybug wings.

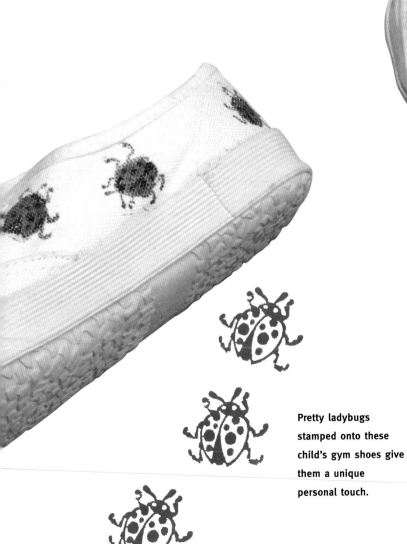

**Pretty ladybugs stamped onto these child's gym shoes give them a unique personal touch.**

# CHILD'S DUVET COVER & PILLOWCASE

*Stamping is an ideal way of decorating children's rooms and works on everything from furniture to curtains, walls, and bedlinen. It can accommodate their changing interests from animals and birds, to fantasy figures and sport, taking them from a nursery to a teenage pad. These sun, moon, and star stamps look delightfully bright and cheerful printed on a plain white duvet with sheets and a printed pillowcase to match.*

MATERIALS
*
White duvet cover
and pillowcase
*
Sun, Moon, and Star
Cluster stamps
*
Fabric paints:
*blue, yellow, red*
*
Red fabric ink and
ink pad
*
Smaller roller and
paint tray or plate
*
4 sheets of plain
white paper
*
Stamp cleaner

## PAINTBOX

There are many different fabric paints on the market suitable for the duvet cover, pillowcase, and sheets readily available in most art and craft shops. Fabric inks are also suitable for the duvet cover, but for larger motifs fabric paint is more vibrant. To match the duvet cover, the pillowcase is printed with the same stamps and in the same colors – but to add interest, the stamps are printed closer together. Always check the manufacturer's instructions – the paints used here need ironing on the reverse side of the fabric to set them.

**1** Wash the duvet cover to remove any sizing. Iron and spread out on a flat, even surface. Make a number of stamped motifs on plain white paper first. You will need to print at least fifteen, cut around them, and arrange them on the duvet. When you are pleased with the arrangement and they are evenly spaced, remove one at a time and stamp.

**2** Pour the yellow and blue fabric paint into paint trays or onto plates, and pour the red fabric ink onto the ink pad.

**3** Apply red fabric paint to the center of the Sun stamp with a brush, dabbing it on lightly.

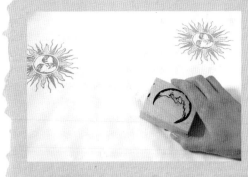

**4** With the small roller, apply yellow fabric paint over the entire surface of the sun, including the red middle. Stamp firmly onto the duvet cover. Stamp all the Sun motifs, re-applying fabric paint each time. When you have stamped six suns, clean the stamp with stamp cleaner to maintain a clear image.

**5** Apply blue fabric paint to Moon stamp with a clean roller and stamp firmly onto the duvet cover between the suns. Reapply fabric paint for each motif and, when you have stamped six, clean the stamp with stamp cleaner to maintain a clear image.

**This duvet cover and matching pillowcase, festooned with suns, moons, and stars, will delight any child.**

**6** Apply red fabric ink to the ink pad, massaging it in well. Ink the Star Cluster stamp and stamp stars in the center of the Moon. Check the paint manufacturer's instructions as the duvet may need ironing on the reverse to set the fabric paint.

**7** Wash the pillowcase to remove the sizing and iron flat. Use the stamp motifs that you cut out for the duvet to arrange on the pillowcase as a guide to printing. Stamp using the same colors and methods as for the duvet cover.

Stamping is especially
fun for children, and
they can help with ideas
or the stamping itself.
You can stamp jolly
bedlinen, T-shirts, and
gym shoes, and make a
child's room lively and
interesting. In this
room, zebras stamped
on the wall add to the
decorative effect.

Looking forward to the
arrival of a new baby is
the time for planning a
delightful nursery. A
cradle looks wonderful
when stamped, and a
blanket and pillow can
also be stamped to
match. You can vary the
cherub motifs or use
them with other images,
as in the mobile.

# CHILDREN'S PARTY

MATERIALS

*

All-purpose craft

glue

*

Used trial-size paint

jars

*

String

*

Scissors

*

3 pots of fluorescent

paint (non-toxic) in

green, yellow, and

blue

*

3 small craft

paintbrushes

*

Napkins

*

Paper plates

*

Paper cups

*S*tamping is an easy and ideal way of making your own party accessories. You could stamp a special theme – bold, colorful animals, jolly clowns, or sparkling stars – or the children could choose their own idea and help with stamping. Fluorescent paints add to the appeal.

## PAINTBOX

Water-based fluorescent paints are readily available in most craft stores and come in a variety of colors. You should always use non-toxic paints and check the manufacturer's instructions carefully before use. If there is any doubt whatever about toxicity, use solely for decorative purposes and not for food or drink.

## TO MAKE THE STAMP

**1** Apply craft glue to the lid of a used paint jar. Cut a piece of string 3in. (7.5cm) long. Place one end in the center of the glued lid and wind outward until you have a spiral shape, and cut off any remaining string. Repeat with another lid and string. Using the same method, wind the string onto a paint lid into a triangle shape. Repeat to make a second triangle.

## CUPS

**1** Paint the rim of the cup with red fluorescent paint and a craft brush.

**Simple fluorescent shapes stamped onto children's party cups.**

**2** With a craft brush, apply green fluorescent paint to the spiral shape.

Easy enough for children to stamp, these decorative party napkins and plates are stamped with fluorescent paint.

**3** Holding the cup firmly, stamp the green spiral onto the side of the cup. Re-ink the spiral and stamp a second green spiral on the opposite side of the cup.

**4** With a craft brush, apply yellow fluorescent paint to the triangle shape.

Hold the cup firmly and stamp the yellow triangle between the green spirals on one side. Re-ink and stamp on the other side.

## NAPKINS

**1** Paint the edges of the napkins in red fluorescent paint with the craft brush.

With a craft brush, apply green fluorescent paint to the lid with the spiral shape.

**2** Stamp the spiral onto the napkin close to the red edge, pressing firmly – try this out first on a piece of scrap paper. Re-ink the spiral and print around the napkin, leaving a space between each motif large enough for the triangle.

**3** Apply yellow paint to the lid with the triangle shape. Stamp between the green spirals. Repeat on the plates.

# CRADLE

*The urge to decorate when a new baby is due need not be confined to walls and curtains. This cradle and quilt use the traditional blues and pinks, but are a far cry from the pale pastel shades. The cradle has been given a simple blue paint finish, creating an almost translucent pearly effect, and was then stamped in a dark pink. The same finish could be applied to a child's bed.*

## PAINTBOX

Two coats of dark blue-green latex were used to paint the base coat of the cradle. The stippling on the panels was done with diluted latex, colored with acrylic paints. When this was dry, a coat of matte varnish was applied, tinted with raw umber, to give it the subtle color of a duck's egg. The struts are painted with a translucent water-based paint which allows the base color to show.

### MATERIALS

*

Baby's cradle

*

½-gallon (2.5-litre) can of blue latex

*

1 pint (½ litre) translucent decorative paint

*

Paintbrushes: 2 1in. (2.5cm) decorator's brushes; I fitch brush; 1 artist's sable or synthetic, size 4

*

White latex paint

*

Acrylic paints: *phthalo blue, raw umber, white, permanent rose, burnt sienna*

*

palette knife

*

Small roller and paint tray or plate

*

Mineral spirits

*

Matte varnish

*

Oil paint: *raw umber*

*

Stamps: *Cherub and homemade star*

*

Medium and fine sandpaper

**1** Protect the floor with paper and apply two coats of blue latex paint, leaving the paint to dry thoroughly between coats.

**2** Stir the translucent paint well before use. Apply one coat of paint to the struts – the areas surrounding the panels. Faint brush marks will be visible. Leave to dry.

**3** Mix 2in. (5cm) of phthalo blue paint with 1in. (2.5cm) of raw umber, and blend with a drop of water and a palette knife. When mixed, add to 1 pint of white latex paint and stir until distributed. Dilute with 2 tablespoons of water.

**4** Dip the fitch brush into the latex and stipple on a spare piece of paper to remove some of the paint. Now stipple onto the side panels, inside and out, and the back and front. Leave to dry.

**5** Mix 1in. (2.5cm) of raw umber artist's oil paint with a drop of mineral spirits, mix well with a palette knife, and add to ½ cup of matte varnish. Apply one coat to the side, front, and back panels of the cradle. Leave to dry.

**6** With the size 4 sable/synthetic artist's brush and the paint mixture used for stamping, paint a thin line along the edge of the top and bottom panels.

**7** Mix 3in. (7.6cm) each of permanent rose and burnt sienna with 1in. (2.5cm) of white acrylic paint. Mix well with a palette knife. Apply the paint to the cherub stamp.

**A delicate paint finish provides the perfect backdrop for this cherub surrounded by stars.**

**8** Stamp the cherub in the center of the top panel. Reapply the paint and stamp the cherub onto the center of the bottom panel. Before stamping onto the cradle, try out on a piece of paper to check the coverage is even.

**9** Apply paint to a small homemade star stamp with the small roller. Try it out on a piece of scrap paper first.

**10** Stamp a number of stars around the cherub on the top and the bottom panels of the cradle. Stamp the stars at random, but fairly evenly spaced.

# BABY'S QUILT

*Stamp this exquisite quilt for that very special baby. Dainty hearts and birds printed side by side create a design reminiscent of patchwork onto exquisite cream silk (I used pintucked Chinese silk). Fine enough to be handed down for generations, you will be stamping your own heirloom.*

## PAINTBOX

Fabric felt-tip pens work well on this quilt, giving prints of just the right delicacy. They dry quickly and will not fade; they need no heat setting and are washable. Most important, they are non-toxic. Another bonus is that several colors can be applied to the same stamp.

## TO MAKE THE QUILT

The quilt here measures 12 u 21in. (53 u 30cm) to fit the cradle on page 118. If you are using your own cradle, you should measure the inside length and width and cut the fabric accordingly.

**1** Cut the silk and the pre-quilted cotton fabric to fit the cradle, with ½in. (1.25cm) to spare on all four sides. (See the diagrams in the template section.)

**2** Measure the four sides of the material, add the figures together, and add a further 8in. (20cm) to obtain the length of lace you will need for the edge.

**3** With the right side up, pin the lace around the edges of the silk, matching the raw edges and making small pleats at each corner, ½in. (1.25cm) in from the raw edge. The lacy edge should be pointing toward the middle of the

quilt. Baste in place, making sure the lace lies flat, and remove pins.

**4** Place the cutout cotton quilting over the silk and lace, right sides together. Pin three sides, two long and one short side, and then baste in place, leaving one end open.

**5** Turn inside out and check that the lace is lying flat, particularly around the corners. If you are satisfied, turn it back again and sew the silk, quilting, and lace in place. Leave one end open to turn back.

**6** Turn the raw edges of the fourth side in, and sew together.

## MATERIALS

*

½ yard (46cm) cream

silk

*

½ yard (46cm) cream

pre-quilted cotton

fabric

*

3 yards (2.28m)

eyelet lace edging

*

Cream sewing thread

*

Pins

*

Sewing needles or

sewing machine

*

Fabric felt-tip pens:

*mustard, turquoise, old*

*rose*

*

**Stamps:** *bird and*

*heart, heart and*

*flowers*

**1** To remove the sizing, wash gently in a washing powder or liquid suitable for delicate fabrics. Follow the manufacturer's instructions for silk. Dry flat and do not iron. Place on a firm, even surface.

**3** Stamp these motifs onto the quilt. To avoid changing stamps constantly, print a line at a time of the same motif. Print side by side in a line inside the diamond shapes. Re-ink the stamp for each motif.

**2** Using turquoise fabric felt-tip pen, apply ink to the heart and flowers on the heart and flowers stamp.

Using mustard fabric felt tip, apply ink to the bird on the bird and heart stamp. Try out first on a scrap of silk.

**4** Apply old rose fabric felt-tip pen to the heart and flowers stamp. Try it out first on a scrap of silk. Re-ink stamp for each motif.

**5** Stamp onto the quilt side by side, along the line above the previous motifs.

**Delicate hearts and birds were stamped onto Chinese silk to make this beautiful baby's quilt.**

# TEMPLATES

*The templates shown on the opposite page are for the homemade stamps used to decorate the file and the large pitcher. The diagrams on pages 124 and 125 show you how to construct the firescreen and how to assemble and sew the quilt.*

# Sun and Stars

FILE (see page 34)
Sun and stars (full size)

These templates can be traced onto paper.
The sun stamp can be made from rubber-
backed felt or high-density sponge. The
method is the same for both materials – see
homemade sponge stamps on pages 17-18.
The stars stamp is made from an ordinary
rubber eraser. Trace the design onto the
eraser and cut out around the star motifs with
a craft knife, so that the motifs stand clear of
the base of the eraser.

   This sun stamp can also be used for the
mirror (page 74).

# Hearts

LARGE PITCHER (see page 100)
Hearts (full size)

Trace the two heart shapes and transfer them
onto paper. Cut them out and place them on
top of the sponge. Dampen the paper hearts
slightly to make them stick to the sponge, so
that they stay in place. Then cut out the
sponge stamps with a sharp pair of scissors.
Sponge stamps are particularly suitable for
curved surfaces, such as on this pitcher,
because they can be "molded" around the
curve.

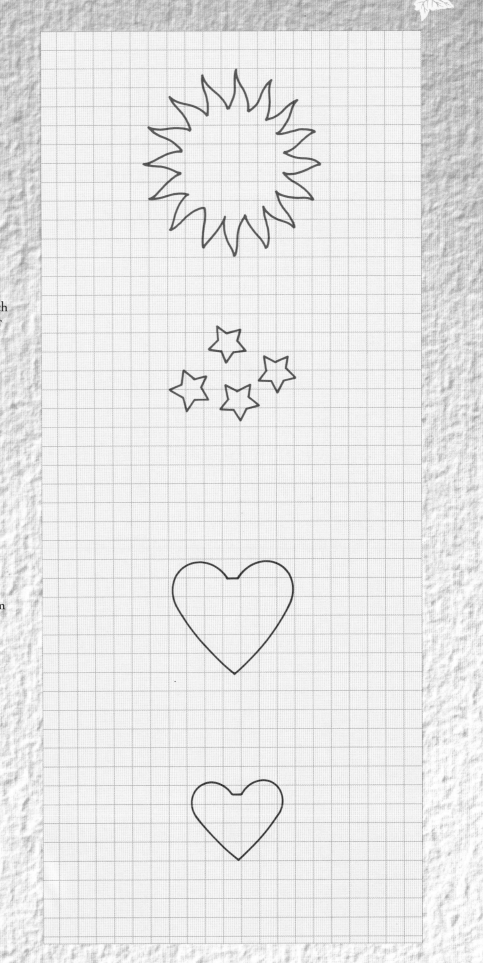

# FIRESCREEN

FIRESCREEN (see page 94)
Diagrams to show construction stages

Follow the steps outlined on page 94 carefully. Fold the sheet of brown paper in half and draw on the shape of the firescreen (*1*). Then open out the pattern (*2*) and place on a sheet of composition board. Secure the paper and draw around it. Cut out the firescreen, following steps 2 and 3 on page 94. Copy the pattern for the back supports (*3*), using the measurements shown. Glue both supports onto the back of the firescreen (*4*).

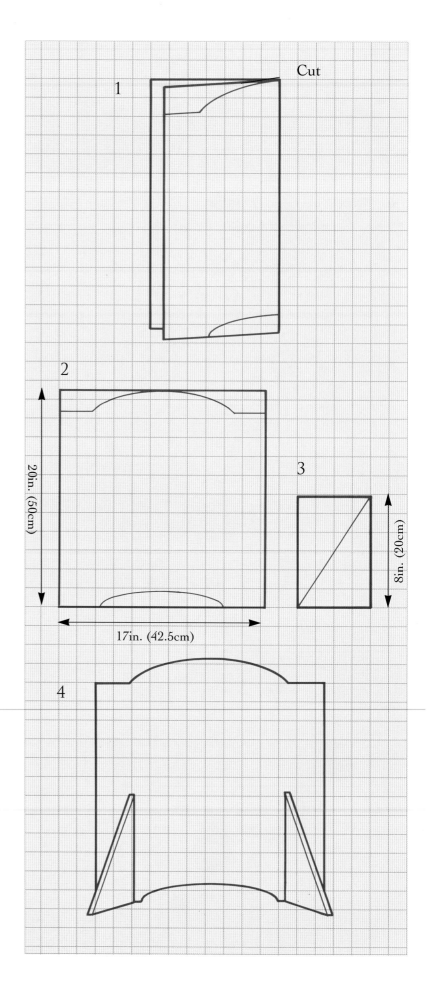

# Baby's Quilt

BABY'S QUILT (see page 120)
Diagrams to show how to assemble and sew
the quilt

Follow the steps outlined on page 120
carefully. With the right side up, pin the lace
around the edges of the silk, making small
pleats at each corner (*1*). Baste in place. Place
the cutout quilting over the silk and lace,
right sides together. Pin three sides (two long
and one short) and baste in place, leaving one
end open (*2*). Sew in place, as described on
page 120.

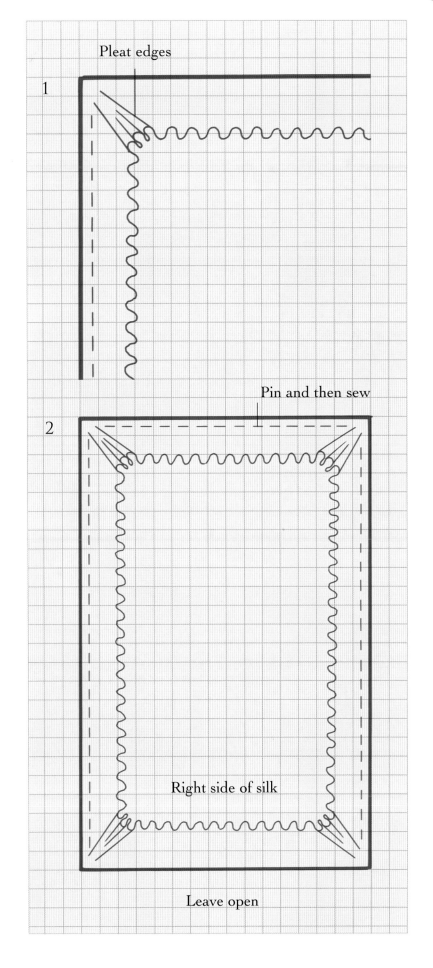

Pleat edges

1

Pin and then sew

2

Right side of silk

Leave open

# INDEX

✦ ✦ ✦

Page numbers in *italics* refer to illustrations

# CREDITS

✴ ✴ ✴

Quarto would like to give very special thanks
to Peter Jones, Sloane Square, London
SW1W 8EL (tel 171-730 3434), who
generously supplied all of the furniture,
fabrics, clothing, kitchen and other equipment
for the book.

We would also like to give very special thanks
to Personal Stamp Exchange, 345 So.
McDowell Blvd, #324, Petaluma, California
94954 (tel 707-763-8058, fax 707-763-7476),
who supplied all of the stamps, paints and
inks, and other stamping accessories for the
book.

Cari Haysom and Quarto would like to thank
the following for their help: The coffee table
and the baby's cradle were specially made by
Stephen Keats. For all of the sewing projects,
we had the help of Judith Myers and Zoe
Campbell. Thanks also to Teresa Daniels, Bill
Edmunds, Mike Hadley, David and Carole
Knott, Simon Waites, and Natasha Walker.